A. DONALD DAVIES

ADVENTURE IN RENEWAL

MOREHOUSE-BARLOW COMPANY
NEW YORK

14 East 41st Street, New York, N. Y. 10017

SBN 0-8192-1170-2

Library of Congress Catalog Card No. 74-80384

Printed in the United States of America

FOREWORD

THIS BOOK is about the education of adult Christians. It is written at a time in the Church's history when a ground swell for renewal is being experienced. The author is a bishop who stands in the traditions and the teachings of the One, Holy, Catholic, and Apostolic Church. He is a bishop who has deep convictions both about Christian renewal and the educational task of the Church. *Adventure in Renewal* is viewed as the primary concern of the Body of Christ as it assists and supports the committed in their Christian pilgrimage.

Adults are expressing a genuine hunger for nourishment in the spiritual life. They manifest the desire for adequate preparation and training for their ministry as the laos, the people of God. While the parish's educational emphasis is on the nurture of children, the Church is called anew to recognize that the growing need of classes in religion for children and young people cannot be met without deeply committed and well trained adult communicators of the Christian faith. The Church's failure to take seriously this ministry with adults continues to weaken the whole Body. Indeed, our inability to agree upon the Church's mission and to evidence genuine concern for outreach in society has its roots here.

A bishop in the Church of God, among other roles and functions, is the Chief Teacher of his flock. In exercising this vital aspect of ministry, the eagerness and the need of the Church's adults has become more and more apparent. The title of this book, *Adventure in Renewal*, was seized upon by a large planning group in the Diocese of Dallas (laity and clergy) as indicative of what we deemed to be central to our task, that is to assist fellow churchmen in deepening the roots of their commitment to our Lord and Savior Jesus Christ. The response to adult education classes offered by the Cathedral Center for Continuing Education has been overwhelming. But local congregations, priests and laity, must be served as well. *Adventure in Renewal* takes book form to help leaders to arrive at an understanding of the theology and fundamental principles of the Church's ministry to adults. The first four chapters attempt to set forth these principles as they are related to the concept of renewal in the parish. The second half of the book is a Manual, containing some practical recommendations and guidance in organizing adult ministry at the local level. These chapters contain approaches both old and new. Several sections are revisions of works no longer available. Help in working with adult education committees and planning programs is constantly in demand. The inclusion of the recommendations in these chapters is in response to the Church's plea for concrete guidance.

The author has arrived at his understandings and convictions in the field of adult education through a myriad of learning situations in which he has been taught by his fellow churchmen. My indebtedness first of all is to the Episcopal Church for the broad experiences provided me in serving as executive secretary of the Adult Division of the National Department of Christian Education. In this respect thanks go to my many colleagues in that department, both on the official staff and throughout the nation, in particular to my partner, Dr. Emma Lou Benignus. I recall with thanksgiving the two priests in whose memory this book is dedicated, the Reverend John Midworth and the Reverend Charles D. Kean, both of whom gave so much of themselves to ministry with adults. Also, I remember gratefully the congregations I served in Kansas and Louisiana, students in my class rooms in the armed forces, in the university and in the theological seminary. In all of these experiences one fellow learner has endured and continues to support my teaching efforts —my wife, Mabel. Without her encouragement this work could not have come to pass.

It is my fervent hope that in a small way this book will be helpful to the Church and will lead Churchmen under the guidance of the Holy Spirit to pray—LORD, REVIVE THY CHURCH, BEGINNING WITH ME.

Dallas, Texas
1974

+A. Donald Davies
Diocese of Dallas

CONTENTS

INTRODUCTION: MANDATE FOR RENEWAL

For reasons beyond our understanding God in His love has willed the creation of a person. This person is made for God eternally, and the first part of his eternal life is to be passed in the probationary school of a finite existence, in which he is to begin to know, love and serve God. His whole life, so considered, is to be in fact a "religious education" that must last from birth to death, continued in ways beyond our knowledge when this life ends . . . all human life is educative in God's purpose. Men here are pilgrims, set to learn on their journey that which they may more fully worship and adore at journey's end.

Reginald Lumb – *The Education of Souls*

IN GENERAL, the Church is engaged in an adventure in renewal. In the search for a clear statement of the mission of the Church in the 70's, churchmen have begun to place the highest priority on adult education. Twice within the past three decades, I have seen the Episcopal Church called to recognize the need for a deeper concern for adult Christian nurture.

Call number one came in 1945 when the House of Bishops expressed concern over Christian education and asserted its influence. The result was the launching of "the new curriculum." Dismay had been voiced over the loss of so many people after Confirmation, over the seeming spiritual unpreparedness of men in the military in World War II, as well as the gross misunderstanding of the place and purpose of the Sunday school. Wisely, emphasis was placed first on adult Christians. Parish life was examined in terms of the process of redemption. The parish, the redemptive community, began to discern its nurturing function and responsibility. Resources were produced to assist the adults in understanding the Church and the Gospel. Six volumes of a teaching series were published and meant to be basic resources for teachers and parents: *The Faith of the Church, Chapters in Church History, The Worship of the Church, Holy Scriptures, The Work of the Church* and *Christian Living*. Through parish life conferences, parish missions, redemptive life conferences, and other similar means, church leaders became aware of both the need and the potential of educated adult parishioners. The Church's education program, however, had always been oriented toward children. Soon out of a sense of guilt or a growing anxiety over accomplishing the overall goal, a shift of emphasis took place: resources and money were channeled into producing a new child-oriented curriculum. Had the Episcopal Church been patient and committed itself to adults for a longer time, the results would have been much different. The direction taken in the development and use of the new series would, in my opinion, have been changed radically and made more effective.

The work with adults started with people where they lived—in a workaday world with its demands, problems to be solved, needs to be met, and decisions to be made. The intent was to discover the freedom and power of the Gospel speaking to man's concrete concerns. The Church's doctrine, body of witness (Holy Scriptures, Church history, *etc.*) and resources (Worship Service Books, Hymnals, *etc.*) then support personal experience and understanding of who our Lord is and what he does in life. The emphasis on the parish as a redemptive community became and remains significant in the understanding of curriculum. In fact, Christian life itself is the Christian's curriculum ("the course to be run"). Curricular tools are the accumulated resources of the Church, attesting to the experiences and commitments of Christians past and present.

The approach of working with Christians "where they were in life," however, seemed to many to be too much shaded or influenced by John Dewey's educational philosophy. Most members of the Episcopal Church continued to evaluate learning in terms of "what I was taught as a child" (or "was not taught"). A narrow interpretation of the godparent's vow in Holy Baptism (1928 *Book of Common Prayer*) prevailed: "Wilt thou also on thy part take heed that this Child learn the Creed, the Lord's Prayer, and the Ten Commandments, and all other things which a Christian ought to know and believe to his soul's health? Answer: I will, by God's help." Curriculum, according to this understanding, was viewed as a systematic exposure to and assimilation of Christian heritage and teachings.

What the Episcopal Church wanted, it got, for the most part. The result was the production of a curriculum skillfully ordering portions of doctrine, Holy Scripture, Prayer Book, Church history to meet and enrich the needs of children and young people. The beginning point was basically the Church's heritage, even though important contributions were made in the understanding of the growth cycle and age-level characteristics. While the intent of the editors of the new curriculum may have been to deal with life's issues first, this was not the approach yearned for by most clergy and lay teachers. Even those courses written to measure up to the curriculum philosophy in adult education were used as vehicles of indoctrination. Dressing up old approaches, using new design techniques and art work, adopting a newer methodology, incorporating a fresh understanding of Scripture—all resulted in the production of an attractive, fresh (and somewhat overpowering) new curriculum. At long last the local Episcopal parish could boast about its educational materials. Nationally, the Episcopal Church could take its place in the educational field along with (if not out in front of) Baptists, Presbyterians, and Methodists. However, the influence of the new curriculum waned as the national Department of Christian Education decreased in importance in the mid-60's, when the attention of the Church became focused on the urgent social and political issues of these turbulent, divisive years.

The curriculum issue is still at the heart of the process of Christian nurture. While the above may well be an oversimplification of one writer's estimate of events and process, one fact must be clear, however: the Church in the 1940's and 1950's, out of expediency and pressure, failed—missing the mark in its nurturing ministry. Missing the mark then has caused the Church to express its anxiety and need once again for the 1970's. Hauntingly, a quote from a document entitled *Toward Redemptive Life* serves to summarize this point.

"If the job of Christian Education is to make Redemption real so that through a new relationship with God the deepest needs of our lives are met, something more is needed by the Episcopal Church than some new Sunday School lessons. If the secret of the power of the Christian religion to help us is found only in a new, living, personal relationship with God, then it is clear why our religion is meaningless to so many Church members. Our Christian Education has been contented to give a very superficial instruction in a few isolated facts about religion. It has done little to create this needed living relationship with God. The life of redeemed relationship cannot be learned merely in a Sunday School class. Redemption is learned by sharing in the redeeming relationships within a truly Christian home and within the life of a truly religious parish family. The Sunday School is only a supplement to both of these. The real job of Christian Education is to help Episcopal families create the relationships of a truly Christian home and the leaders of parishes to create truly Christian relationships among its members. By living and sharing in these Christian relationships day by day, year by year, children and adults find religion meaningful and the help it gives them real."

Another crisis in the Episcopal Church also caused a sudden shift in its educational task. The General Convention of 1967 redirected programmatic interest and funds. Concerns for the disenfranchised, the powerless, and the minority members of society became the issue at that Convention. Since the curriculum is the Christian life, the needs of fellowmen presented the Church with a religious issue. Indeed, the curriculum issue. What really is our responsibility in terms of mission? Where does it begin? The mission fields once so far removed (and always ready for harvest) were now made distant by the Convention's program only by emotion and commitment. More immediate neighbors were looking to the churches for imaginative expressions of Christian mission and a practical proclamation of Good News. Thus, the prophetic became paramount in program. Impowerment was outreach; enablement, mission. The Church's program began to take on endeavors and ministries for which most churchmen had no frame of reference in experience. Work was being carried on in all segments of society and not necessarily with fellow churchmen or for the purpose of winning the powerless and minorities to our membership rolls. Much of this had been seen as a vital need in the *Mutual Responsibility and Interdependence in Christ* program with outstanding results. But in MRI, most of the involvement was with companion churches of overseas jurisdictions. The discontent, furor, and reaction to the self-determination programs of and with minorities were evidenced in many ways. Mistakes were made both in the philosophy and in the administration of the program. But the new directions for ministry and mission, although at times disturbing and upsetting, did make an impact. The Church which once assumed leadership in Christian Education now had prophetically become involved in the kingdom's ministry to a changing, freeing-up society. While some aspects of the General Convention Special Program could have been effected differently, there is no doubt that the Episcopal Church had responded eagerly and conscientiously to what it believed to be God's Will.

Call number two came when the Executive Council of the Episcopal Church, in 1970, inaugurated an Office of Development. Its objective was to ascertain what the Episcopal Church conceived to be its basic mission in the 1970's. A systematic visitation of the dioceses became an important resource. The highest priorities expressed were: (1) Christian education for adults, (2) Evangelism, (3) Renewal, (4) Meeting the needs of others, and (5) Communication.

The Executive Council interpreted this expression of priorities in a report entitled *What We Learned From What You Said.* In part, the response stated:

Response: A very clear pattern emerges from the diocesan statements. With few exceptions, there is almost total agreement that a major change in emphasis is desired in the General Church Program. This does not appear to be primarily a negative reaction to present programs, but rather a positive call for response to other fundamental needs within the Church and her members. Apparent throughout the statements is a consciousness of a spiritual awakening, both in and out of the Church, which has evoked a strong individual and corporate desire for growth in the life of faith, education in Christian thought and viewpoint, and guides to involvement with the world. There is a deep desire to know Christ and to be involved with others. There is an expressed need for training in the skills and disciplines that nurture us in Christ and that enable us to make Him known to others by both word and life style. Believer and non–believer need nurture and conversion.

The need expressed is for personal and corporate spiritual renewal, for knowledge and growth in "the faith," for help in learning how to reach out to others—to meet both their spiritual need for the gospel and the social and economic needs which justice demands. Thus education, spiritual renewal, evangelism and social action are all seen to be interrelated, each dependent upon and growing out of the other.

Why did adult education receive the highest priority rating? The reasons are many. First, the variations between dioceses and within dioceses and the varied experiences of the participants would dictate a variety of responses. An understanding of the implications of this ranking is necessary. Some kind of judgment will be used in determining the meeting of this priority in the Church's program and budget for years to come.

What *did* the Church say in designating the phrase "Christian Education for Adults" as a number one priority? What is valued and sought after? Could it be that "the curriculum issue" is involved?

There are at least five possible expressions of need being voiced. For convenience these may be phrased:

Recover the Disciplines
Father, Teach Us
Back to the Bible
Train Us
Toward Renewal

1. *Recover the Disciplines.* A desire is being expressed for a maintenance of a worship life. The disciplines conducive to spiritual growth have been neglected. The offering of our adoration and praise to Almighty God has always been central to our community. The significance and beauty of the worship of the Church need to be reemphasized. The spiritual disciplines of prayer, meditation, private devotions, and the sacramental life need to be recovered.

2. *Father, Teach Us.* In a day when traditional values are being questioned, churchmen need to know more about the Church's beliefs and teachings. This is a time

for sure direction. Christians have received a magnificent heritage. Sadly, many adults know little about the Church and her teachings. Since one of the basic functions of the Church is teaching, the role of the priest or minister as teacher and communicator of the Faith must be recovered.

3. *Back to the Bible.* Since many view the growth in numbers of the "conservative" churches to be a result of their emphasis on the Bible, it is not surprising that the more "liberal" churches should express the need for Bible study. The entire Church comes out of the Bible and should remain deeply engrossed and oriented in the drama of God's action and revelation. We have an increasing need to hear the Holy Scriptures and to "read, mark, learn, and inwardly digest them."

4. *Train Us.* One suspects that this need arises out of the inability of persons to function well as Christians in the world. Discipleship, evangelism, and the exercise of leadership are part of renewal. These functions do not automatically emerge as a result of Baptism or Confirmation, although the responsibility for them begins there. The Church needs to understand not only what should be taught or communicated but also *how* to teach it. The failure of many parts of the Church to be totally and wholeheartedly engaged in a prophetic ministry is rooted in the fact that people don't know how to be either priestly or prophetic as Christians in society. For this, training and discipline is called for as a part of renewal.

5. *Toward Renewal.* Elements of the above four needs certainly must be involved here; indeed they must be met in any proposed approach to Christian education. It would be hoped that the majority of adults would have a basic yearning for a deeper relationship with our Lord and Savior. An adventure in renewal is an adventure of commitment to the Lord of life. In a troubled and difficult lifescene isn't there a power and relationship which strengthens, gives hope, and saves? That relationship makes sense out of the non-sense in life through the presence of Christ Jesus. The plea for high priority for adult education provides direction and definition to the word curriculum. Toward renewal is the recovery of meaning and resources in the lives of adult Christians.

There may be many other reasons for the selection of adult education as a number one priority. The above is merely an approach toward understanding some of the main ones known to the writer.

In response to the visitations of dioceses, the Executive Council of the Episcopal Church studied and analyzed the data received. The Council's statement of what was heard reveals something of the old cries for help as well as the hope for better approaches in meeting this objective. Sixty-seven of the dioceses asked for a new and innovative program of Christian Education and fifteen others wanted substantial revisions in the existing program, indicating an almost unanimous demand for a greatly increased educational emphasis.

> The kind of program envisaged is a comprehensive one including all age groups. It would have its first and strongest expression at the adult level. It would be related to and help empower the new and vigorous ministry being sought by the laity. It would reach out with consultants, skills, and direction to youth and those involved in higher education. It would concern itself with the worldwide mission of the church and would be the interpreter and kindler of our social concerns. It would be oriented toward diocese and parish. It should make maximum use of all media, not all of its efforts going into the traditional alone. Material and approach should be more flexible and versatile than ever before, particularly as regards both size and cultural setting of the church addressed. The Program should run the gamut of motivation, communicating skills, producing materials, *etc.* Its point of entry must be at the adult level. A large sum of money is clearly called for to implement this first priority. It will take several years to staff and begin the actualization of such a program. (From, *What We Learned From What You Said*)

Summary: The Church is engaged in an adventure in renewal. Twice within the last thirty years the Episcopal Church has been called to educate her adults. The Christian education of adults has been given the highest priority for her mission in the 70's. As a background we have surveyed the Church's struggle with the curriculum issue. At what point do we begin to educate adults? Do we begin with the Church's teachings or with the adult's chief resources, that is the life he is living? The failure to deal realistically and forcefully with this issue in adult education in the forties has deprived the Church of much of its spiritual vitality and vision. Such failure directly influenced the production of material for children and its use in the churches. Content-oriented education did not meet the needs nor bring about the kind of God-man relationship which evidenced itself as the concern of churchmen. Will we repeat this error or will the Church engage the issue with all its resources?

Adult education has become the highest priority in the Episcopal Church for a variety of reasons—as varied as the dioceses and diocesan leaders who contributed to the scoring or rating. Nevertheless, there exists *now* a sense of motivation among adults for a genuine learning experience. *How* that motivation will be met or understood is yet to be seen. One thing is certain—adult education will be a major enterprise and, it is to be hoped, a renewing force for the years ahead in the Episcopal Church.

1. LEARNING TO BE THE CHURCH

The Christian Gospel is Good News, not just in the sense of pleasing information, but in the more dynamic sense of effective transformation. When the notes of the Gospel are struck in such a way that people can hear them and respond, God's purpose for men, both as individuals and in society, is fulfilled as far as we can understand what fulfillment means. Striking the notes of the Gospel effectively is the task of the Christian Church as a whole, and in this task the local parish church finds the justification for its existence.

Charles Kean — (*The Christian Gospel and the Parish Church*)

THE CHRISTIAN GOSPEL is *the* dynamic answer to the sense of lack that all men have. The Christian Church exists by God's grace to proclaim this answer to all men and women. Through the acceptance of what God has done and is doing in their lives, they may be enabled to find meaning in life and to live creatively amid its problems.

This chapter is intended to deal with the fact of man's need and God's redeeming action. Any adventure in renewal must begin at this point. Renewal is a recommitment. To what does the Christian need to be recommitted?

The use of the word renewal indicates some lack or deficiency and an expression of need. It follows that whatever might fulfill this sense of incompleteness would indeed be "good news." Such news would give meaning and purpose to a life formerly devoid of direction. One can stake one's life on the validity and the authority of *the* answer given by God himself. To what kind of lack is the good news addressed? What are the aspects of human existence to which the Gospel of Jesus Christ claims to be good news?

Since the Church's function is to proclaim the Gospel to all people, obviously we must start with those for whom the communication is meant. Thus, we begin with men and women who either have never heard of God's action in their behalf, or having heard do not understand and cannot accept it as *the* answer for their lives. People must be convicted before they will be committed to anything beyond themselves. They must be made aware of both the need of more in life and their inability to satisfy that need through their own resources. They must come to recognize their need for:

freedom and power in living,
help to deal with life's persistent problems,
joy in living and facing each day,
understanding reality and having the strength to live with it,
purpose and meaning for existence,
knowing themselves and others,
assurance that somebody cares.

On the other hand, they know all too well frustration, aloneness, despair, separation, torment, selfishness and meaningless.

Unless the good news of the Gospel is heard, this predicament remains. Men and women continue to pass through life unfulfilled as persons. The task of the Church is to communicate, to proclaim, to broadcast this good news. An old definition of Christian education takes on added significance here. For both the purpose of the Church and Christian education must be the same, namely: to proclaim the Gospel to all people with such clarity and in such a way that children, young people, and adults may hear it, accept it, respond to it, and be transformed by the power of Christ. When the Gospel is proclaimed and accepted, then can begin the pilgrimage of becoming what God means each person to be—redeemed, a free person, a child of God, an inheritor of the Kingdom of Heaven.

Many years ago the Episcopal Church approached adults with this message in a document entitled *Toward Redemptive Life.* An excerpt may indicate how right and contemporary that call to action and renewal was.

DO YOU NEED REDEMPTION? What is modern life like—in relatively comfortable America? Nearly everyone we know carries a heavy burden of worry and nervous strain. One out of ten is spending time in a mental hospital. Many are seeking psychiatric help. Children are insecure and nervous. Home after home breaks up in divorce. Moral standards, even in high places, have become confused. The strongest of us have to do constant battle to make sense out of the world in which we live.

Truly we need salvation from the frustration and confusion of modern life. We need relief from the increasing nervous tension that builds up within us. We know that our own inner resources are not strong enough by themselves to help us very much. The harder we strive to be calm, the more troubled we become. The more we tell ourselves not to worry, the bigger our worries grow. The more we try to relax, the more tense we find our nerves.

We all need a strength and spiritual power greater than our own. The Church is here to show us how to find that greater strength. The Church is here to help us learn how we can have this spiritual help. Before we can have the saving help, however, we must know what God has done to give us this great gift. The story of what God has done to help us is called in theology, *The Drama of Redemption.*

Perhaps you have been a little bit afriad of the word "theology." Like many modern people, it may be that you have favored what is often called "a practical down-to-earth religion." This usually means a religion that helps you know right from wrong and which tells you how to get along with other people. Let's be realistic. Can a religion composed mostly of moral teachings really do for you what needs to be done to give you inner peace today? Our real trouble is that we feel so frustrated and so separated within ourselves and from other people. A religion which tells us merely that we ought to live the right way isn't very much practical help. What we really long for is to be united with something the modern world cannot shake or destroy. We long to find an inner peace. We long to rid ourselves of an inner feeling of loneliness and separation. No amout of being told that we ought to be decent and good is able to do this for us.

This is where a little understanding of "theology" begins to help. This inner state of loneliness and frustration is called "sin" in theology. Before sin is an act, it is always a condition within us. Try as we will we cannot get rid of these feelings by our own efforts. *The Drama of Redemption* is the story of what God has done to make it possible for us to be freed from this inward life-destroying state. The Good News of the Gospel is that salvation from sin is a free gift from God.

(*Toward Redemptive Life*, p. 4 ff.)

The divine drama of human redemption can be passed off as only an historical account of God's acts, all of which are contained in the Holy Scriptures. (See the Appendix for a chart and description of the Drama.) We are not Christian because we believe in the historicity of the events in a story; we are Christian through our acceptance of God's action in sending his Son, Jesus Christ, and thus accepting the God of the drama. We are Christians by our decision to live in a restored relationship rather than in a state of separation, to live in obedience to the will of God rather than our own will. We are Christian when we share the saving acts of God within the Gospel community—the Church. For the life and worship of the community of the redeemed becomes the locus where we recognize ourselves as sinners and draw upon grace as we are sustained in the community of the people of God.

The Parish Church, a Redeeming Fellowship

The parish is not dead. It is a viable entity. It will survive. It is the concrete expression of a group of Christians in a certain geographic area. But more, the parish is the place where Christians identify with the One, Holy, Catholic, and Apostolic Church and have opportunity to live out the Gospel. It is a faith or Gospel community. It is effective to the extent that the nature of its "community" manifests what it professes. Is the parish church the place where the healing of brokenness and separation is evidenced in and through its worship and activities? Do the members view its chief function to be the ministry of reconciliation in a broken world? Is it involved in the restoration of man to God and man to man? Do people seek out the parish church as a place to be at one with God and to draw upon his strength? To what extent does a particular parish manifest excitement and conviction in participating in the divine drama of human redemption? Is it known for its loving concern for people and for its assiduous efforts to make known the good news in the broken social and political community in which it exists? In other words, what does life as it is lived in the parish tell about the good news proclaimed and the nature of the members' commitment to God's mission to men?

The parish church is a community of neighbors gathered about the altar to celebrate their redemption. Its nurturing function is an important part of its life. This is not to imply that Christian education is going to save souls. It is rather to state that the nurturing process is a vehicle to assist the committed Christian to deepen his life in the faith through experience and understanding. Its purpose is that the Christian may more deeply glorify God and be a more effective channel of his redeeming grace, both within the parish and in the world about him.

If this is true, the adult educational program of the parish faces a threefold test. First, does the Gospel, as it is mediated through the life and organizational efforts of the parish, make a difference *now* in the lives of people? The good news is not primarily that man, when he dies to this time-space existence, will enter into life everlasting. It is, rather, that here and now, in this life, man can begin an eternal relationship with God. Christianity is not a preparation for the future; it is living now in Christ. Christ died for me that my life may be joined with his life now, continually now, at every moment of my existence. This means that every activity of parish life is a proclamation of that truth. For instance, when Mrs. McDonald participates in a Women's Lenten Study Class, is she helped to see that God's redemptive grace is at work in that class, as it comes together, and in the very process of learning? If this is not so, can we justify a study class which ignores the central truth that it is *now* that God speaks to each of us?

The second test to which an educational program must be subjected is: Does that program speak to the *whole* person? The Gospel speaks to the whole of life; all creation has been redeemed. When a man attends a men's club meeting, he brings with him, as part of himself, his relationship with his family, his concerns in the community, his working experience. All of this is part of what makes him a person.

Our society and to a large extent the Church has tended to atomize people. The Rotary regards a man as a community-minded person, industry as a producer, political forces as a voter, a fellow worker as a competitor, a neighbor as a golfer or bowler. The parish church has tended to regard him as a canvasser, a men's club member, an usher. The Gospel speaks to him as a person who, like all persons, lives in a complex of relationships and participates in a complex of functions, but who is a whole person, created in the image of God. In this way, the educational program of a parish must see him.

His main areas of relationship include his family life, his political life, his work life, his social and community life and his leisure-time life. These are the areas where he makes his decisions, where the Gospel has meaning, and where by his decisions he witnesses to his faith. The same is true of the women, and, to some degree, of the children.

Further, every person has certain ever-present needs which we might call persistent life problems. They, too, are complex and interrelated. Adults have a need for security, peace of mind, a sense of well-being. They have physical and emotional needs—for adventure, for new experience, for meaning and value in life, for self-realization, and for feeling that they are expending their talents and gifts to the fullest. Unless the parish educational program assists adults in experiencing God's response to these needs, it is failing its objective. When adults participate in a study group, Christian education takes place if the relevance of the Gospel is understood in these terms.

A third test asks if the *whole* parish is seen as the educational force in the lives of its members. The Church is the channel of God's redeeming grace. It is not just the sacraments, nor the parish suppers, nor the church school, nor the fellowship, nor the Bible; it is the whole parish through which Christian education takes place.

This presents two difficulties. The first is the need to overcome the tendency to fragmentize people through parish activities. An accepted pattern in the past separated men from women, children from parents, older people from younger people. This has some merit, but the parish easily loses sight of its essential unity. A woman's guild can exist almost unrelated to a men's club or, for that matter, the rest of the parish. The young peoples' group may have no vital relationship with the activities and associations in which parents of the teenagers are involved.

We can test this further by its effect on the family. Concerned as we are about the solidity of family life, are we at the same time being a divisive influence by separating members of a family when they participate in the life of the parish? Bill goes to the Men's Club on Thursday night, Mary to the Guild on Tuesday afternoon, and Ella to the Young People's Group on Sunday evening. Are they being led to see the relationship between these activities, as it is set forth when they all come together to worship as a family on Sunday morning?

Consideration of this leads us to the second difficulty: How can we integrate the many educational thrusts which take place in the parish? Organizations, study groups, sermons, tract racks, parish library, social gatherings, informal meetings—all are part of the educational life of the parish. Through all of these the Gospel must be communicated—whether it be an understanding of the imperative for mission, a clearer realization of the relevance of Holy Communion, or a more profound recognition of the heritage of the Church as it reveals the will of God to man today.

As we deplore fragmentizing the family in the parish, so must we strive to avoid fragmentizing the faith. To do so is to deny the unity of the Gospel. For instance, for Bill and Mary to learn about the mission work of the Church only through pre-canvass publicity is a denial of the wholeness of the Faith. Corporateness of parish life is more than occasional manifestations of good fellowship. The Body of Christ indeed has many members, and each part has its peculiar function, but equally important is the fact that every part is a member of the same body, existing and functioning for the whole. Through the organizational and educational life of the parish, the adults should become aware of this.

Christian education can lead adults to understand and

experience the reality of the Christian Gospel in their lives at every moment, speaking to each as persons and as part of the larger fellowship. This is a tremendous task. But the Gospel is *the* tremendous fact of life. The parish church exists to do that which the Gospel demands of it. By the power of God and always under his judgment, to strive for this is our only choice.

In viewing the parish as a redemptive fellowship, let us explore briefly the investments and expectations the adult brings with him from "his world out there." When we survey the multitude of activities in which he engages, we find there are certain basic categories. In these realms he makes his most important decisions. In order to make the decisions, he searches for guidance and support. The decisions he makes affect his deepest relationships. Every decision in every aspect of life affects his relationship with God. Also, each decision strengthens or weakens his relationship with his fellowman. Accordingly, the areas of life where decisions are made are the places where the meaning of the Gospel is most clearly encountered.

For the twentieth century Christian, there are four major areas of decision. These four, far from being clearly marked off, are, to a great degree, overlapping areas of relationships and creativity.

FAMILY
WORK
COMMUNITY
LEISURE

1. *Family.* This is the blood family, the closest of human ties and responsibilities. The adult is related to the family as son/daughter, husband/wife, or parent. Basically, the adult exercises his responsibility to those who are dependent upon him not only for shelter, clothing, *etc.*, but also for guidance, love, and concern. In this realm the adult's motives and convictions are exposed and best known. Decisions made here affect both the immediate and future relationships of each member.
2. *Work.* Here we are concerned mainly with vocation and the endeavor to earn a living and provide

for those for whom the adult is responsible. For the man, this is his daily toil and business enterprise. For the woman, it may be the same as the man or it may involve a vocation as housewife and mother.

3. *Community.* Including the local and worldwide aspects of communal relationships, this area involves man's attempt to live within community. This is mankind organized for the common welfare, security, education, and for survival. Here the adult accepts responsibility in a variety of groupings: P.T.A., service clubs, school boards, National Guard, Red Cross, Scouts, Little League, political parties, housing issues, racial issues, *etc.*
4. *Leisure.* This area involves the where, how, and with whom the adult spends "free" time, that is, time not committed to pursuing a livelihood, caring for a family or maintaining community. A person's attitude toward leisure has a significant bearing on whether he or she is creative or not. The growing leisure orientation of our society due to shortened work weeks, lake homes, boats, ski trips and the like, poses a problem for the Church in the maintenance of the norm of parochial life. The "lexodus people" (leisure-exodus on weekends) will be part of our culture from now on. Will the Church be able to break traditional ministry patterns and accommodate this apparent need?

The ability of the Church to explore new patterns, in some respect, is being dictated by the current energy crisis. The lexodus people are called upon to reassess priorities. For many, a careful examination of schedules, patterns of participation in events/activities and an evaluation of goals is called for. In this regard, the energy crisis may bring relief to an activist society. Increased concern for church attendance and participation in the Christian fellowship may also be one of the fruits of the crisis. However, the Church must be ready and willing to explore new ways to meet the needs evidenced by our desire to be "recreated" in leisure opportunities.

In these constellations of relationships the adult searches for understanding and selfhood. These four areas press all men for decisions, whether they are pagans, agnostics, or Christians. What makes the difference for the Christian? What is the place of the Church in relation to these constellations of relationship and areas of decision making?

When the parish church is seen in its proper perspective, our diagram would appear like this:

```
                P
               FAMILY
             WORK
        COMMUNITY
            LEISURE
                H
```

Although somewhat contrived, the diagram does serve to make an important point. The Church is not and cannot be viewed as another competing organization or institution within the framework of a community. It is more correctly, by its very nature, *The Community* which supports and sends forth Christians strengthened to work and witness in the world.

Learning to *be* the Church is not something that can be either programmed or scheduled on a timetable. Nor does all the training take place under the roof of the parish church. This kind of training is the Christian's life style, and it takes place in two different ways simultaneously:

1. Within the fellowship and security of the parish family,
2. At the frontiers of society.

The ongoing process of the adult's involvement in Church and world takes place through a sort of rhythm. First, there is the ingathering, the coming together as a parish family. Here we celebrate our redemption and are fed by the grace of God. Then comes the scattering, the "going abroad" to our various stations and callings, where we are to live by that which we have received in the strengthening fellowship.

At these frontiers, where we try to live as Christians amid conflicting values and demands, we stand a chance to discover anew the power and the truth of God. It is here that we are tested as we dare to share the gifts we have received. Here, we test what we have learned and experienced about forgiveness and grace. Here, also, our discovery of their validity will carry its joyous message to the world. From such experiences, we need to return to the parish altar and friends, to share our discoveries, recount disillusionments and successes, receive renewed strength, cleansing and refreshment so that we can go forth to try again to live as though we *really* belong to Christ. In this living rhythm the mission of the Church is being carried on. By taking part in it we become educated in the ways of the Lord.

Summary: The Gospel of Jesus Christ speaks to man's basic needs, redeeming him and giving him power and freedom to live creatively amid life's problems. The proclamation of God's action for man's salvation is the good news of the Gospel. Moreover, it is not just God's *historic* action, but his *nowness* that man experiences. The drama of redemption is lived out in concrete ways within the parish church, the community of the redeemed. The function of the parish is to support and sustain the people of God. It is a channel for the Gospel. The nurture or education in the faith of the people of God takes place in all that is done in the church-gathered. Formal opportunities for growth are only a minor aspect of the maturing life of adults. Thus, central to renewal is the appraisal of the kind of life lived within the faith-community. Evidences of the quality of commitment and the depth of the Christian's sharing in the ministry of reconciliation will be manifested in his life beyond the parish house doors as he is involved in sharing in God's mission among men.

2. ELEMENTS IN RENEWAL

Christian Education for adults is a dynamic interaction between the Word of God and the situation we face. There will always be a tension between these two forces, or the temptation will be to avoid the conflict by making God the object of study or domesticating Him. If we start with God, we must move to consider Him in the light of our present situation. After all, nothing is real until it is local. If we start with our human situation, we must move to God who is "standing watch above His own." Regardless of starting point, if we have a fruitful conversation between the two elements, we will help our adults come to a personal knowledge of God, an understanding of His will, and a determination to serve His cause.

Dr. C. Ellis Nelson, from "The Divine Constraint of Christian Education for Adults."

THE PARISH is, essentially, a spiritual community which, constantly, is drawing its strength from the presence of Christ in its corporate life and which is turning outward to bring its redemptive power to bear in the world in which it lives. Organized ministering to the members of this community and to their witness in the world may be referred to as the church's program. Basically, the church's program is the Gospel and its function is to set forth the Word (pro-gramme). Participation in and acceptance of the program makes demands on everyone in the parish. In fact, endorsement of the program carries with it certain responsibilities and privileges. Christians are called upon to proclaim the good news by word and deed, to open the hearts and minds of men to hear and accept the claims of Christ, and to provide ways through which people can have a living dynamic experience of good news.

The need is not that men have religion but that they be religious. A religious person is aware that God is present and confronts him directly through the hour by hour experiences and decisions of life. A religious man is able to respond affirmatively to God in crises rather than to himself. To help men respond like this, parish leadership is called upon to plan for the adult's education.

The Christian's growth is a lifelong process. In this respect, it is helpful to draw a distinction between adult Christian education and the education of Christian adults.

Adult Christian education encompasses those activities and experiences which are educational by design and intent and which result in formal programs under guidance. The education of Christian adults, on the other hand, refers to all those influences and experiences within parish life and beyond that have an impact on the adult and help him become a more responsible and responding

Christian. These include classes and programs, of course. But the education of Christian adults has to do with the total experience of living. It refers to the need to assist the adult to interpret and evaluate his responsibilities and to deepen his self-understanding in the light of his commitment to Christ.

Implementing this commitment involves three elements, each dependent on the other. An examination of the elements may provide us with a clearer understanding of the educational implications of the Church's ministry.

1. **The Church is called upon to provide opportunities within the parish to assist the adult to become a new person in Christ through confrontation with the Gospel.**

It has been said that religion is caught, not taught. Commitment comes as a result of a relationship with the Lord. Such a relationship does not come through a study course, that is knowing "about" the Lord. Study may deepen one's understanding, but when that happens the study is only fortifying the commitment already made. To be confronted with the meaning and power of the good news involves wrestling of the soul. Man sorts out his personal goals, desires, and needs in light of God's offer of a life of freedom and power. The parish fellowship must offer people opportunities for experiencing redemption and renewal in their relationships with their Savior and with one another. Through opportunities to be involved with fellow Christians in Christian living, the adult will discover ways of responding to God's offer of love. As indicated in Chapter One, the quality of life within the redemptive community, the Body of Christ, is at the heart of the adventure in renewal.

While programs and formats may assist in achieving this element of growth and renewal, these must be considered only as vehicles. The term vehicle is used rather than method or tool. A vehicle is something that assists the user to move in a definite direction and is always available to serve additionally as needed. There are many tried and proven vehicles to assist the adult in his spiritual pilgrimage. Some, because they have been used in other eras, are mistakenly considered outdated or useless for contemporary use. Retreats, quiet days, and preaching missions are in this category. Imaginative and creative work is being done, however, in these areas in many communions. The old Ignatian retreat format (a series of meditations and periods of silence) still serves well for some. Combinations of the old and newer methods have been very helpful and well received. One thing they have in common is providing skillful guidance in reflecting and wrestling with oneself in relation to one's loyalty and response to the Master.

Bible study can also be useful. There is a growing desire for an understanding of the Holy Scriptures. The neglect of this part of the community's life causes many people to run hither and yon in search of help. The Church has preached and set forth liturgically the centrality of the Word of God. It is time that the Church demonstrates her dependence on this revelation. Bible study sessions and groups may be one way to meet this need. The need served would be informational for the most part. However, another approach may serve a different need. The adult needs to participate, to have the opportunity to share and reflect, rather than to have all the work done for him. It is in this kind of process that he is "stabbed awake" to new and vital truth. God speaks through his Word—we teach and preach. Why not provide people with the opportunity to hear him speak directly to them rather than always through a leader. It is hoped that the method of small group Bible study contained in Chapter Nine will serve to give both adequate direction and the assurance of a proper approach to a learning situation.[1]

2. **The Church is called upon to assist the adult through participation in a variety of learning situations and activities, to grow in understanding of and concern for the nature and heritage of the Christian Church.**

Basically, this element reflects the formal, well organized, academic offerings in adult education. Most adults

1. The material contained in Chapter Nine was originally compiled by the author and the Rev. John Midworth. It has been out of print for some years.

will define education in terms of the activity of the classroom in which we learn about God and his Church. In other words, education in a traditional sense is an effort to seek to acquire skills, knowledge, understandings, attitudes, and appreciations through an organized effort. There is nothing wrong with this concept, as long as it is not the beginning point in the search for a Savior. The good news is not a body of knowledge to be taught; it is experienced first. Once experienced, it can be clarified and its impact deepened in the formal learning situation. The Gospel narratives take on great significance when a person has already become related to the Master, Teacher, Shepherd, Savior, and Healer, whose actions and teachings are recorded by the Evangelists.

The heritage of the Church is of abiding significance. Every Christian ought to know about God's dealings with his forefathers, as well as become familiar with the experience others have had through and after their conversion. A Christian would be an egotist and an ingrate to pass off or to ignore the witness and development of the people of God. Let us agree that the Church's history, sacraments, worship, theology, morals, prayer books, Scriptures, and symbols are on the one hand to be studied and on the other to be appropriated in our own expressions of conviction and belief. The relation of this all-important heritage to the Gospel experience needs clarification.

Some years ago Dr. Emma Lou Benignus and I served in the Episcopal Church's ministry with adults. In an effort to clarify the concepts of encounter with the good news and encounter with heritage, a diagram was designed. Perhaps its use here will serve to guide the reader to a new understanding of this important distinction. Let us compare first and twentieth century Christians.

In the first century, God introduced himself to man in the person of Jesus Christ. The earthly life and ministry of the Son of God was comparatively brief. During his ministry he gathered a small company of ordinary men as his disciples (learners). These disciples had the first-hand experience of sitting at his feet as he taught, witnessing the healing miracles, and having their own lives changed radically. They found new meaning and power for living as their lives were transformed by his presence.

They walked, talked, slept, ate, communed with the good news of God in the flesh. After the death and resurrection of Jesus Christ, through the power of the Holy Spirit, this small group of followers became apostles, those commissioned with a message. The Apostles and growing company of the Way began to bear witness to the one who had transformed their lives. The results of their sharing may be diagrammed thus:

1st Century

JESUS CHRIST

↓

The Experience of Good News

↓

Heritage
Scriptures, O.T.
Gospel narratives
Symbols (art forms)
Prayers
Liturgies
List of Saints
Sacraments
Ministry
Creeds, *etc.*

The believers felt compelled to share, to communicate their at-one-ness with God and how the good news was available to all. What was experienced *inwardly* was now to be expressed outwardly. What we call heritage was the outcome of their efforts to verbalize what they had known. Thus, they prayed in certain ways, worshiped corporately differently in various locales, ordered portions of teachings in Gospel accounts, sacraments and later credos. What we have included in "heritage," therefore, is really a record and explanation of the transforming experiences of others and their responses to the new life in Christ. An important body of informational witness!

Now, one step further. As stated above, knowledge will not save us. Many make the mistake of believing that mere saturation in the heritage will bring about the same experience of good news which transformed the first century brethren. Certainly the heritage can awaken us to our need and point us to the Way.

First Century		*Twentieth Century*
JESUS CHRIST		BODY OF CHRIST
↓		↓
Experience of Good News		Experience of Good News
↓		↓
Heritage resulted	⟶	Heritage

However, the mastery of the subject matter of the faith can never substitute for having faith in the Master. At best, involvement with the experience of other Christians will provide a vivid account of what is possible when a person comes into the hands of the living God. But it is imperative that adults have the opportunity for the adventure themselves. The first-century Christians had a firsthand relationship with Jesus Christ. The twentieth century counterpart of his first century presence is the Gospel community, the Body of Christ. The quality of life lived within the Body of Christ must show that the good news is being experienced.

When something of the Gospel becomes real and meaningful in life, then the teachings and witness of others become a potent resource. They reflect and symbolize what is now known firsthand. The creeds, hymns, and Scriptures became our own. We discover within the ancient words, phrases, and statements the power to interpret our own lives. Thus, we discover and appropriate to ourselves what the Church in other eras had known and described in formal communications. They are no longer voices from the past inspiring us, but rather we are inspired because we are able to use the same language and the same words to describe what we know and are.

Thus, programs with adults will continue to teach the Church's heritage. They will also take into account the climate of relationships in which the learning takes place. This is where the language of relationships becomes the content of the faith. Certainly, no one can program a Gospel experience for someone else. We can, however, provide the kind of supportive, challenging, and concerned environment in which the Holy Spirit is free to move.

3. **The Church is obligated to enable the adult to respond to and participate with the community of God's people in fulfilling the mission of the Church to all mankind.**

Sharing the gift received through work and witness is a necessary response by anyone who has been given the secret of abundant life. The redeemed one becomes part of a missionary society. In response to the gifts and power given, the testing as well as the nurturing of the relationship to Christ is to be shown in the manner in which the person now assumes responsibility for others. So the Church gathered for worship and nurture responds by extending the fellowship into the world where men suffer and stumble. The expression that this outreach and witness takes will be in large measure a reflection of the depth of the redeemed one's understanding of sacrifice and being Christ's man for others.

The three elements of program are important directions in planning to meet adult needs. While each element can be understood as being a part of the overall program objective, a word of caution is called for. It is impossible to isolate any of the above three elements of renewal, excluding the other two, without the result being an inadequate ministry. Yet, there are many evidences of inadequate programs being built around the learning of facts, or total emersion within the problems of society, or entrenchment in a constant revival atmosphere. Each to the exclusion of the others—with one of the elements becoming the complete activity. Such one-sided efforts, however self-pleasing to the leadership or comforting to the people, are the reason for much of the discontent with present educational situations and approaches (or their lack). There is mounting evidence to indicate that care and planning for the education of children that has been lacking is also lacking in our work with the adults. Efforts to educate en masse have been exposed as a weak and incompetent endeavor. Even the secular world has learned this hard fact. To persist in such efforts bespeaks a misunderstanding of how the three necessary elements are related to the day by day life of the Christian adult.

Summary

The elements in renewal are many and as varied as the multifarious interests of the participants in adult education. The Church has a mission to teach, to bring the message of God's love to bear on the situation in which man finds himself. Three elements for renewal may be considered as part of a whole. While each can be examined, together they comprise a guide for planning a well-balanced ministry with adults. Briefly the elements provide for commitment (renewal) in Christ, understanding our heritage, and involvement in outreach and witness. The proposal of the three infers their inclusion as one objective in planning. The comparison of first and twentieth century Christians describes the relation between the two languages through which we communicate the Gospel—the language of relationship and the language of words and symbols. Both are important to our task. The distinction will aid in placing the proper weight and emphasis on the elements necessary in adult endeavors.

3. A COMMUNITY OF LEARNING

Learning is change. There is no teaching unless there is learning, and there is no learning unless there is change. This means not only the change that comes from more knowledge, but also change of attitude, change in ways of believing, thinking, perceiving, acting and doing. In Christian Education we seek to have changes take place as a result of the teaching-learning process. We want those whom we teach to change in the direction of Christlikeness. Persons do not become more Christ-like except as they come to know Christ as Lord and Saviour and grow by grace and by the work and power of the Holy Spirit into His likeness, so that the Christian who is growing is the one who is in Christ.

Training to Teach, Harry and Betty L. Goodykoontz

We have discussed the foundation for renewal, the place and function of the redemptive community, the parish, and the elements necessary in a ministry with adults. Now, let us turn to a consideration of the adult himself as a learner or participant.

It probably has been the experience of every priest

or minister to have adults express a desire to have a "class." One wonders at times whether the response to inquiries or surveys on adult interests doesn't reveal the expected "church response." This is to imply that adults may give back exactly what they feel is being asked for. Still the majority of our adults probably respond out of genuine need and with every intention of participation. But why don't they participate when the offering is finally made? In this chapter, we shall discuss some convictions about adults. In particular, we shall examine certain observations as to why and how the adult will "sign up" and participate eagerly in a learning situation.

Conviction 1: ADULTS MEASURE UP TO DEMANDS, DESIRE ACHIEVEMENT

Learning requires hard work, concentrated application, and time. The adult takes seriously a commitment when made. In every other aspect of life he is confronted with requirements, rules, and guidelines. He either abides by that which he has accepted as normative or strives to change it. Are justifiable demands made upon him by the church, especially in an educational society? One suspects a hesitancy to impose requirements for participation. One also suspects that many adults view the activity to which they are being invited as on the same level of professional seriousness as many religion classes for children.

A task without genuine demands and requirements has little attraction for adults and doesn't call forth their best efforts. Leaders need to be reminded, however, that demands made on participants require the ability of the leadership to produce in direct proportion to what is being asked for.

Two illustrations come to mind, both of which are parish experiences. One is in a college parish situation, the other a large suburban parish. In each situation the rector was known to the vestry and people as a good and experienced teacher. The vestry in the college community comprised twelve men, each holding an earned doctorate. This body requested the priest to conduct an adult class on the Bible during Lent. It was hoped that at least the vestrymen and their wives would attend the class. Three

Sundays before Ash Wednesday the rector made the announcement, laying out the schedule, but more important, the conditions. These included a commitment to attend every session and to read all the portions of Scripture assigned prior to each class. The vestry's reaction was that the priest had limited severely the number who would attend, even from within the vestry. The result, however, was startling. Over one hundred came, attended each session, prepared the study assignments, and entered wholeheartedly into the learning process. The same was the experience in the large suburban parish, with an even larger number and a request that the class go on for three more weeks. In that situation a small fee was charged.

What came out of these experiences was a great sense of accomplishment both for the participants and the teacher. A success experience is essential to the educational process. Pride may be dangerous, of course, but someone has said that the pride of achievement can be of value, if the sense of achievement is confined to the spiritual welfare of the group.

Conviction 2: ADULTS RESPOND TO SHORT-TERM STUDY

It is the author's experience that the adult's interest and participation run high when the number of study sessions on a given theme are few. Few, in this regard, refers to from three to six sessions, compared to a year-long, week by week adult class. The limited number of sessions does not preclude the possibility of the participants electing to pursue the subject for more sessions than originally scheduled. The point is that just as the course grows out of the expressed concern of the adults, it is the adult members who elect to continue.

The short-term concept has merit in that more adult issues and concerns can be considered. It is possible to offer several courses or units at a given time or schedule them throughout the year. The nature of the liturgical year provides many possibilities for study schedules. Epiphany, Advent, and Lent, for example, present not only the perfect time factor (three to six weeks), but the sense of readiness and expectancy necessary to learning. It should be noted that the demands of adult education, like the demands of the faith, involve a year round program. The hit and miss pattern (spurt and sputter system) with its occasional adult offering is grossly inadequate.

Although the adult may not enlist in every opportunity for educational encounter, frequent and varied opportunities need to be made available on a regular basis. The mobility of our people and the leisure-mindedness of our culture are factors contributing to the value of the short-term system. Another aspect of enlistment is the definiteness of scheduling. Adults respond and participate more fully when they know exactly when the class will begin and when it will end. This principle applies both to an individual session as well as to the series. (One reflects on the number of adult "continuing" [weekly] groups and how one almost had to die to be released from attendance or guilt for absences.) When a series is announced for four weeks, consideration of its value and the adult's availability will determine the participant's enrollment. He knows also that he is free to leave the group at the conclusion of the fourth session without feeling like a dropout. With this freedom to fulfill an obligation comes the high possibility of future commitment according to interest and need. Enlistment is commitment. Enlistment denotes a high degree of interest to participate and to accept the requirements, anticipating at the same time the prospect of growth built into the course design.

Conviction 3: ADULTS WHO SHARE PARTICIPATE

When the adult shares in the planning of the program, he is more likely to participate. Such sharing in planning involves helping to select the theme, arriving at the goals and the selection of the procedures or methods. There is a direct relationship between the extent of involvement in planning and commitment in the program itself. Effective planning creates a setting in which learning, personal development, and adjustment in intergroup relations can take place. Planning is a learning experience in itself. Imposed or already designed programs brought in must be sold to a group on their merits or on the ability of the leader to inspire loyalty to the program and/or himself. The merit of participation in planning is that the investment of opinion, interest and concern assures a sense of investment in both the ongoing class and its outcome. Maximum responsibility for the determination of the activity must rest with the group members. Since the Church is a community, its activities and programs are properly of a corporate nature, not only in their execution, but in their origin and planning as well.

Conviction 4: ADULTS DEMAND VARIETY

No one approach, technique, or method of teaching has proven to be the panacea for all program ills. For lack of imagination we usually have tried to settle on one or two methods, for example, lectures or movies. Variety in the study methods employed is just as essential as offering a variety of opportunities for study. Adults differ greatly one from another, by reason of background, education, experience, and temperament. Such differences call for the leaders and planning members to be acquainted with the rationale behind the use of numerous methods (vehicles) and procedures designed to move the group along toward a desired objective. Whereas one method may be the best procedure in one phase of a program, it may be the poorest and least effective to employ at another time. The nature of the issue under consideration, the aim in coming together, the resources available, and the physical facilities are factors determining the method that can be used most effectively. In Chapter Eight detailed consideration is given to the principles of program planning.

Conviction 5: CONSIDER THE ADULT FIRST, "GROUPING" SECOND

In every parish there are certain recognizable groups: young adults, parents, teachers, leaders of study groups, men's groups, women's groups, young marrieds, golden years. Each offers an opportunity for growth and, therefore, makes demands for program. These groups deserve both attention and assistance.

However, when the ministry of these special (functional) groups becomes the major emphasis of the parish program, the result is the effective fragmentation of the parish family. It has also brought into being a host of independents or nonjoiners who by their own choice stand outside of any organized program. Although functional groups within the parish are important, our plea is to approach the adult first as a child of God who is in need of a Savior; minister to the responding and functional ministries of groups second.

Parents, young adults, the aged, are all adults. They have many of the same spiritual needs, ask the same piercing questions, and face similar struggles and temptations of the soul. Differences in age and experience obviously require consideration. But we cannot continue to put parents into one group, young marrieds or unmarrieds into another, "senior citizens" into still another, when all have much to share and to learn about the Christ. We must approach people as persons, not as functions. Let us provide every opportunity for grappling with the meaning of life and renewal of commitment to our Lord before proceeding to these special areas in which men respond and witness in society.

The very nature of the Christian faith provides us with the basis for our approach to adults as persons. The revelation of God through his Son stands at the heart of our being and, consequently, at the heart of all that we undertake. Our insights and convictions come by revelation. It is the Holy Spirit who conveys the truth of the faith to man in life's experiences. The age of the adult is not the key factor. The real problem is human sin—sin which leads people to resist the Gospel and to live to themselves. The "Good News" is that through grace people can become different persons. They can be transformed by a power greater than any human effort and be recreated in the image of Christ.

The key to understanding adulthood in the Church is to be found in the Gospel itself. It was to adults that the good news first came. And it was adults who accepted joyously the responsibility for conveying and communicating the Gospel message to others. From the standpoint of function, priority, motivation, and responsibility these children of God are unique in the Church, both past and present.

Summary

The Christian adult is not only capable of learning, but desires to be part of the learning experience. Why, then, do so many act to the contrary? Allowing for physical and personal commitments, are there other reasons why there is a reluctance on the part of adults to be engaged in learning? We contend—we must know the adult. Not by studying his maturing characteristics and ability to learn but by examining the conditions which may provide the kind of freedom the adult needs for participating in Christian nurture. In other words, what will it take to get adults into a learning experience willingly and expectantly, guaranteeing free, full participation? Under what conditions will an adult sign up, continue in the process, participate creatively, and ask for more? The conditions covered are concerned with the person as a contributing being. Gifts are to be brought, shared, and honored. Therefore, we must consider what are the justifiable demands that can be made, the quality and benefits of short term or long term programs, the adult's privilege and responsibility to share in planning, the variety of approaches, and the adult as a unique person apart from his natural/functional groupings.

4. THE PARISH—TRAINING GROUND FOR RENEWAL

The objective of Christian Education is to train the Church to be the Church, the Community of God's People through whom the Holy Spirit, if He wishes, may make Himself known in the world. Jesus of Nazareth was the Incarnate Body in whom God revealed His living power to men in Palestine. Now the Church, made up of clergy and the laity, is the living Body whereby this same Spirit becomes known among men today. It is necessary, therefore, that we who are a part of this Body know and love God in every way possible in order that we may be used by Him for His purposes. The mission of the Church is to be of service to God as He calls men to repentance and to reunion with Him. He has made it very clear that those who would serve Him do so by serving the world around them. As we see it, the clergy and laity, together are the Community through whom the Holy Spirit can work to draw the world back into relationship with God for which it was intended. The parish Church ideally is the training ground where with guidance and support we can help each other to learn to be the Church. Dr. Emma Lou Benignus

FOR THE faith community, the Parish, education takes place not only in guided and formal learning occasions, but also throughout the whole of parish life and activity. The purpose of this chapter is to review the training opportunities for men and women in the average parish church. An adventure in renewal may be to some the call to seize upon a new program. "When will the answer (study course) for renewal be ready?" As indicated, however, renewal is first and foremost the determined effort to recommit the believer in relationship with our Lord, and then a recommitment with fellow believers to the Lord's work and mission. Since the arena of this activity and expression is the parish, an examination of aspects of parish life reveals abundant opportunities for growth and training, some of which may have been overlooked, some of which may need "redeeming." These are considered under four general headings: worship, organizations, formal study, other educational channels.

1. *WORSHIP*

The offering of praise and thanksgiving to him who is worthy to be praised is the central activity of the Christian Church. "My duty as a member of the Church is to follow Christ, to worship God every Sunday in his Church, and to work and pray and give for the spread of his kingdom." It is a privilege and duty for Christian man to acknowledge the "worth-ship" of God. He enters into worship for the purpose of praising and adoring him who gives life, rather than for what he can get out of it.

Since worship is pivotal in our lives, the liturgical services of the Church are indispensable in training men and women for Christian life and witness. We need to comprehend what we are doing, saying, and believing in our acts of devotion. Unfortunately, many adults come to the altar year after year without realizing the bounty of which they partake. Just coming to church is not enough. The people of God need to reexamine their worship life by asking some basic questions: Are the services of the parish meeting the needs of all parishioners? What needs *are* met? How much of God's Word do people in the pews hear through the reading of the Old Testament, Gospels and Epistles? How can people learn to pray consistently and deeply? Why is it that, even though every Sunday Christians hear that their Lord's Body was broken for them and all mankind, and even though they receive his gift of himself, they are still so chary all the week about letting their lives be "broken" or even scratched for others? How is it that they can receive him yet not share him with others through sharing themselves with others? How is it possible that people can receive him for years on end yet not be profoundly changed?

The greatest opportunity for growth in understanding the meaning of worship in our time is the Church's concern for liturgical renewal. Liturgical renewal is the opportunity not only to accept with gratitude our heritage but also to fulfill the demand in every generation of Christians to contribute to that heritage. From an educational point of view, the symbols used in the 1928 Book of Common Prayer of the Episcopal Church are largely words that express the understanding and beliefs of the agricultural, low-profile industrial era of the seventeenth and early eighteenth centuries. A new Prayer Book will include twentieth century expressions, understandings, and beliefs about God and his world.

The merits of the services approved for "trial use" in the Episcopal Church need not be discussed here. For the record, there is a great host of congregations where the contemporary liturgical concern is taken seriously as a means of intelligent and effective response to the action of God in life. New vigor in worship has resulted. The opposite has proven to be the case where the attitude exists: "Why all the fuss? This will pass away." "We will await the finished product before getting involved." In either case, the "new product" will undoubtedly be used as the Book of Common Prayer was used, that is, with little understanding of what it is saying or how it is intended to assist the worshiper. These parishes have missed an unusual opportunity for enlarging and deepening their worship life, as they have also missed the chance to contribute to the process of renewal.

The following suggestions may help a parish do more educating within the context of worship:

1. Provide as rich and varied liturgical worship as Worship Service Books, the Church Calendar, feasts and fasts, and tradition allow.
2. Use intercessory prayers, prayers of thanksgiving, and litanies in public worship as well as in parish prayer groups.
3. Try instructed worship, especially at Holy Communion and Holy Baptism.
4. Encourage group discussion on the meaning of what we do and what we are as a worshiping community, the meaning of prayer, ritual, and ceremony.
5. Offer instruction in family worship in the home, making creative use of such resources as the Advent Wreath, family prayers, *etc.*
6. Schedule quiet days (or evenings) and retreats, experimenting with new services being used by other liturgically-oriented churches.
7. Recruit and train the laity to assist in public services through reading Scripture, serving, leading intercessory prayer, participating in the Offertory procession, *etc.*

2. *PARISH ORGANIZATIONS*

American churchmen are prone to organize. The existence of organizations within the parish lays before us a responsibility to see that they exist for the right reasons and to assist them to do so. No organization should have its own existence as its chief end or purpose, although many function as though they do. Every group within the parish properly should have two objectives:

(a) Each group is designed to serve the parish in some special way. The particular gifts of many of the groups grow out of their function, for example, the choir, church school teachers, altar guild, vestry, Parish Council or other governing body. They have their specific areas of service and responsibility. They exist to serve the ongoing life of a community. They must be concerned that their efforts parallel the basic objectives of the total redeeming community in ministry.

(b) In addition, each of the organizations has a responsibility to its members, so that their experience within the life of the group will be one in which the power of Christ is known among them *now*. For example, as the choir practices hymns about God's forgiving love, the human relationships within the choir are the opportunity immediately at hand for this segment of the Church to live in accord with what they sing. Occasionally, it might be helpful to discuss the subject of a hymn or anthem. Furthermore, as they sing on Sunday they can mediate God's forgiveness to those in the congregation with croaking voices and tin ears, who in time and with patience might be helped. And so it goes for all organizations.

Parish organizations are training grounds in Christian living. They are miniature communities in which we can practice Christian living. Some day it might be said of us, too, "see those Christians, how they love one another," or—as the young people sing—"They'll know we are Christians by our love." Not until we try to live as devotees of Jesus Christ do we find the demands of such living, the cost and the joy of it. It is only as we risk loving others that we get a glimpse of what it cost God in his Son to love us as he did. It is within the parish group that we can prepare for what it will cost us, his Living Body, to be at work in the world. The place to get our basic training is within our parish family, where our loyalties are shared and where our foibles surprise no one. Whether groups work for the parish in service in the world, or serve themselves in programs of study or prayer, they are always human relations seminars where we can help each other to live freely under God.

3. *FORMAL EDUCATIONAL OPPORTUNITIES*

In our experience, what a parish usually means when it claims to have "adult education" going on, is that it sponsors study groups for adults, such as inquirers' classes, parents groups, Bible study classes, a lecture-discussion series, the Rector's Hour, or the like. Some of these such as the Rector's Hour may function as year-round groups with long-term programs; others are seasonal. Still others arise spontaneously out of a specific situation in response to a specific need. Some of them are formally organized, some are loosely structured; some meet in the parish house, some in homes. Very few of them, except those for parents, are a normal mixture of men and women or a healthy family mixture of young and old.

Whatever their composition, these groups assemble to learn about specifically designated subject matter. A list of courses and study programs useful to us who would like to do an intelligent job of practicing our faith could compete with the course listings in any college catalogue. We can never know enough of the Church's doctrine, the contents of the Gospels, the viewpoints and experiences of the writers of the Epistles, the critical points of Church history, the meaning of the sacraments, the innumerable details of worship, the lives of the saints, the ways of prayer, religious symbols and art, and Church polity. The subjects are endless. Factual, doctrinal, and ritual knowledge is essential in a layman's training. Christians need to hear, rehear, and identify with the detailed heritage of their Church, for this is their culture, and in a very real sense it defines who and what Christians are. They need to rehear the same stories, to listen again to the same teachings and discuss again their meaning. For, after they have heard and lived by what they heard, they need to hear again and then go forth again to live in fuller measure. This spiral of growing and living into the faith is part of the educative process. It is needed throughout all one's years on earth, and especially when life pinches hardest. There is no such person as one who is fully grown in the faith. At best, men and women are growing in trust, love, and obedience. This is not done only by disciplining the will but also by disciplining the mind.

However, factual, objective learning is not enough. Training for adults is not brought into its fullest significance for us until each one asks himself, "Now that I have heard God speak, now that the Church's position is clear to me, what bearing does the Word have on me and my life as I am living it now?" Or, "In light of what I now know about God in Jesus Christ, what must I now be and do?" Irrespective of the importance of their subject,

Christian education courses and programs fall short of their purpose if they do not confront the individual with questions of relevance. We have found that information for information's sake is about as fruitless for Christian growth as are self-centered church organizations.

Relevant learning, or "learning-for-livingful" meaning, is made easier when our human relationships are such that we can afford to face the facts of our lives. For instance, a man hears the preacher say that Jesus Christ died to save sinners. If this man's position in life makes his sinfulness inadmissible even to himself (there are many in this situation), if he must pretend that he is not sinful, he puts himself into a position in which Jesus' dying for sinners has no meaning for him. To the preacher's statement he may well reply, "So what!" No amount of rational argument will convince him to long for Jesus Christ. Only a realization of his need for what God has done and is doing will start him consciously on the route of return to him. Consequently, if there is to be effective Christian education for adults, there must be a milieu in which our courage to face ourselves can grow. We want help in saying, "I have need of what God in Christ has done for me." We also need help in making new responses. The conditions under which we might dare to question ourselves are rightly provided for us in the parish family groups to which we belong. We, in turn, rightly help provide creative relationships for other people. The study group, the Bible class, the parents' class, if these really are the Church, will be the kind of groups which give to all the members support enough for honesty and freedom.

This is why we all need some small group life (See Chapters Six and Seven). Small educational groups and groups which work together are vital to growth in Christian learning. The worship of the whole community on Sunday is an expression of the life of Christians as they live in small "family" groups during the week. One reason Sunday worship does not mean more to us is that we do not see the connection.

Such a supportive Christian milieu provides helpful directives about the size of the group, the nature of leadership, and the methods of group operation. A gathering so large and so formal and so infrequent that we cannot get acquainted is not one to provide the kind of personal relationships helpful for relevant learning. Dominating autocratic leaders usually make us fear for our souls rather than free them. Anxiety provoked by wariness of others seals both the mind and heart.

Where there is significant Christian education going on, two things happen: discovery, or revelation, and change, or response. A person discovers who he is, what he is, where he is now in the light of who God is, what God has done and is doing, and what God therefore would have him do now. Change, or response, issues forth from the wellspring of gratitude a person feels for his discovery. As a man moves toward God in trust and joy and finds that his faith is not misplaced but is answered through the meditation of the Christian body, gratitude can deepen into longing, perhaps even into a burning desire to do his Creator's will rather than his own. Such is the route of sanctification. This is the lifelong process of Christian education. Our part in it is to provide the relationships in which the Holy Spirit may do his work.

4. *OTHER EDUCATIONAL CHANNELS*

Listed below are some channels for adult education in the average parish community. The reader will discern the abundance of the opportunities, even though they are not usually considered educative by nature or design. Nor are they always utilized in the most effective manner as teaching tools when their educational possibilities are seen. The brief statements made here are hardly definitive, but they may provide suggestions for an educative use and function.

Altar Guild. While this is a service group, attention should be given to the personal motivation, commitment, and growth of the members so that they learn to understand why and for whom they serve the people of God.

Annual Parish Meeting. Often required under the laws of the denomination for the transaction of parish business, review of program and expenditures, and for election of officers, this gathering offers unusual opportunities for eliciting interest in and concern for what the Church is all about. Creative and stimulating presentations of parish life and activities are called for. The meeting need not—indeed, must not—be dominated only by the kind of relationships permitted by Robert's Rules of Order.

Daily News. Every Godfearing person needs to learn to read and hear the news (newspaper, television, and radio accounts) in such a way that God's Word to man can be discerned in the events reported. Here is the behavior of the civic community, the drama of human relationships and events which this day have done their best to crush or free man, to build or to destroy God's world, crying out for the Christian's conscience to take a stand. Many a saint has begun his meditations on the meaning of life, of God's love, and formed his intercessory prayer list after reading or hearing the daily news.

Drama. This is one of the earliest organized forms of communication used by the Church to illustrate the great moments in human redemption. Miracle plays, morality plays, marionettes (Mary), Punch and Judy (Pilate & Judas), pageants, reflect the endeavor to use other means than preaching. Today other dramatic forms (movies, television, theater) are available for interpreting the religious issues with which man lives.

Women's Guilds. The women of the Church have consistently stressed study and educational programs. At times, the only program of adult education offered in a parish may be one sponsored by the women.

Every Member Canvass. This organized effort lays before church members the teachings of good stewardship, active participation, and a concern for fulfilling "My bounden duty . . . to follow Christ, to worship God every Sunday in his Church, to work and pray and give for the spread of his kingdom."

Family Life Groups. Here parents or parents and children get together to study society's demands in relation to the function of the family as it draws upon the resources of the Church and in the exercise of the spiritual disciplines.

Instruction in Worship. A formal explication of the action and offering of the people of God is made either in the context of the worship or through an explanation and discussion at the coffee hour or a study group.

Inquirer's Class. The inquirer is a seeker—an adventurer—who commits himself to a series of prepared presentations and discussions of the basic teachings and principles of the Christian faith, and the doctrine, discipline, worship and life of the Church as believed and practiced by the communion he seeks to join.

Leadership Training Class. A special training discipline for leaders in the church school, the church governing board, men's, women's, and youth group leaders, *etc.* The leadership training class is designed to increase motivation and ability to handle communication skills in teaching the faith.

Missionary Education. Church members need to understand the nature and urgency of being part of God's mission to men. Review of where the roots of the Christian faith have been planted and fertilized is not missionary education but missionary information, which may quickly lose its glamor with the turning off of the projector. The missionary expression is out "there," but the impulse to respond in gratitude to God for what he has done begins where we are and then goes forth. We are a people *on* mission.

Neighborhood Groups. In many parishes there are natural clusters of fellow churchmen living in the same neighborhood and meeting for fellowship, study, service, and prayer. All share in the total outreach and evangelism of the local church.

Neighborhood Visits. Is this education? Certainly, if it is more than a call on a neighbor out of curiosity or for gossip swapping. Systematic calling can be the attempt of the Church to show love for the neighbor by both a ministry of presence and shared concern. One parish grew from two hundred to one thousand members in less than a year because it determined to visit and know every neighbor within six blocks of the church. While these visits were not necessarily for recruiting, the response to this expression of caring was overwhelming.

Parish Bulletins. They can be either a great waste of time and money or an enthusiastic bearer of welcome tidings. They can be either mere announcement sheets or an instrument of significant communication. Well-written bulletins with a message will continue to be vehicles used by the parish family for growth and self-understanding.

Parish Family Nights. The gathering of the family for a meal and for fellowship can be a learning occasion as well.

Parish Library. Books on religious issues and subjects belong in every church or parish house. Advertising their presence and worth are important in building or maintaining such a resource. Use of the library can be promoted from the pulpit, and in bulletins and announcements. Basic reference books, commentaries, cassettes, various translations of Scripture, technical studies in education, *etc.* are tools a parish ought to provide its leadership. One important source for the study of religious issues should not be ignored, namely, contemporary novels and best sellers.

Parish Life Session. Opportunities for specific groups (the vestry, for example) or a representative parish group to withdraw and carefully examine what the parish is really doing about its mission and ministry as the People of God can lead to renewed commitment and direction.

Periodicals. There is a dearth of good religious news coverage. Local and national denominational magazines and newspapers attempt to publicize what the Church is doing beyond parish boundaries. The reporting of events and the ministry of fellow Christians becomes a way of sharing the good news and a source of food for thought, action and prayer.

Prayer Groups. Prayer is the real work of the Church. A prayer group gathers together churchmen to be a community of intercessors, for the purpose of remembering the Church's work and workers, the ill and oppressed, the victorious and grateful, and others within the community in their struggle to be Christian in today's world. As a participant, the clergyman can exercise his priestly or pastoral role in response to the need, "Lord teach us to pray."

Preaching and Teaching Missions. These are special efforts to convert the soul through preaching and teaching, a concentration of spiritual endeavor in one place for a short time. Preaching missions are usually inspirational, dealing with the motivations of the individual to participate in the Christian life and mission. Teaching missions are usually informative, bringing new understandings of the doctrine, worship, and teachings of the Church.

Quiet Days. Similar in purpose to the retreat, quiet days are concentrated in a shorter period of time, for reflection, meditation, prayer, and silence. Many busy communities have found quiet evenings to be most beneficial.

Retreats. A retreat is a brief period of time (two or three days) for building up the life of the Spirit. In an atmosphere of detachment from the distractions of daily living, the Christian can deal freely with the disciplines for living the Christian life, growth in the Spirit, and a sense of vocation.

Sermons. The sermon, a verbal proclamation of the Gospel, is intended to give religious instruction, guidance, and exhortation in the Christian life. Pre-involvement of hearers through questions, outlines, or brief statements in the bulletin; sermon forums; dialogue sermons; congregational selection of theme-texts; even group writing of a message—all have significance in assisting in the communication of the Word.

Social Action. Almost every parish becomes involved in responding to the faith by showing concern for the needs of others and offering genuine service. Leaping to serve and ready to act is too often the norm. Learning to serve and being prepared to act comes slowly. Education can help here. We must study in depth not only the particular need to be "serviced" but also our own motivations in acting, the kind of help really needed, and the kind of resource that can best be called upon to assist.

Tracts. Those little leaflets printed in small type which rest on stands in the narthex serve to inform the faithful on important aspects of truth. More than this they should be! Tracts can be creatively used as "one session" study pieces at coffee hours or study groups. Their brevity and conciseness have great merit in this regard, as well as for distribution.

Audio-cassettes, which are available so abundantly, are becoming the contemporary tracts. People are learning to listen again. Cassettes dealing with today's theological issues, Bible study, devotional messages, *etc.*, are on hand and, because of their brevity, can serve groups for study and discussion in much the same way as the printed word.

Vestry. While normally thought of in terms of managers of the finances and property, the vestry's responsibility is to assist in setting the goals for the program of the parish. As such, vestrymen must be intelligent, committed, well informed, *active* communicants.

These are but a few of the opportunities for the utilization of the varying aspects of parochial life for nurturing purposes. The nature of the community of believers should cause us to be ever alert to ways of improving, strengthening, and supporting one another and the whole Body in the process of maturing. The education of a Christian is a community affair; it takes place within community and is a design for community. Is it possible that we know so little of the ineffable joy and meaning of life within Christ's Body because we seldom are challenged to live together in the world as his faithful people? We cannot be the instruments of his peace except as we accept the cost of life with him. Most of us march round and round, as the constabulary in *The Pirates of Penzance,* bravely singing under the shelter of the parish house or the roof of the church, "We go, we go, we go to meet the foe." But then we do not go. As we depend on God (and support each other in that dependence) in our going out from the parish altar to our stations in the world, the strength of his grace becomes known within us.

In the words of Evelyn Underhill, our activities, whatever they are, "matter only because they are a part of his great spendthrift, saving, loving action within life." Through us he can touch, mould, create, transform other spirits. We were given to him in baptism, and we give ourselves to him again of our own free will. "We have to remember all the time that the real point is not the use we make of him but the use he is making of us. For that we go into training."

For leadership and direction in this kind of Christian education we plead for the help of the total Christian community.

5. THE PRIEST, PEOPLE, AND PLANNING

No PRIEST who really listens to his people can doubt that the majority of them, no matter how well educated they are in secular subjects, have only a fragmentary and elementary knowledge of the Christian faith and its practice. The reasons for this are many: inadequate teaching in the church schools of yesterday; no living witness to the faith in most of the homes in which the adults of today grew up; no serious Christian instruction beyond early adolescence; a public school system from which almost all reference to religion is excluded; universities that are secularized; the fact that many adults are half-instructed converts from other communions. Most important of all, perhaps, is the fact that hour after hour, day after day, year in and year out, our secular society is continually educating all of us. Its methods are powerful and varied: movies, television, radio, magazines, newspapers, books, billboards, and all the many forms of advertising. Essentially our secular society presents images of man's nature and destiny that deny, ignore, or are incompatible with the Christian view of life.

If it is true that adults within the Church have an inadequate and confused knowledge of Christian teaching, it follows necessarily that they lack the motivation and the knowledge of how to express Christian teaching in their lives. We must conclude also that, in our age at least, liturgy and preaching alone are not enough to produce informed, convinced, and practicing Christians. The Church and the clergy thus have an enormous additional responsibility and obligation. The Church is the divine institution which is commissioned to proclaim the Gospel of God to all men. It is also charged with the responsibility of proclaiming the saving Word of God to those within its fold. There is no doubt that the Church does proclaim the Word; the real question is *does she proclaim it in such a way or ways that it strikes home to the people she is teaching*? This is a question that cannot be passed over lightly by anyone who has taken ordination vows.

Some supplement to what the Church has been doing for adults in the past is obviously called for. What that supplement should be is clearly indicated both by experience in the Church and in secular life as well. While the huge growth, within the past generation, of adult education classes in secular subjects has been paralleled in some parishes by a very effective religious education program for adults, the Church as a whole has been slow to awaken to this thirst and need.

What has been demonstrated beyond doubt is that adults can learn and that many of them are eager to learn. It has also been shown that adults are not hungry for education simply for the sake of acquiring knowledge, but will participate only when the course deals with material they believe to be of interest to them. This is one of the main reasons why the small reading and discussion group, when properly conducted, has proved so successful—it allows adults to raise questions about real problems in their own lives and to talk over these problems with their friends. No single method of teaching is adequate to the task, however. Adults want and are stimulated by variety, therefore, all sorts of educational procedures should be used.

The rector or pastor of a parish is the chief Christian educator in the congregation. Whatever his training, he has the responsibility for the job. However, to carry on a major and varied year-round program of adult religious education, such as is recommended in this book, is beyond the ability of even the ablest parish priest unless he has strong support from at least three or four of his laymen. There are too many courses to be surveyed, too many books on methods and procedures to be read, too many organizational details for any one person to handle.

Fortunately, during the past ten to fifteen years interested laymen have been found in many parishes who are glad to work at this task with the encouragement and guidance of the clergy. In addition to their ability to help the clergy, the laymen bring another valuable resource to the job—they know the way other laymen think and feel, and they know what interests them.

When a priest says, "Of course you can run a good adult program at St. A's parish—look at all the leadership you have there! Unfortunately, here in St. B's our laymen aren't up to it," he is expressing not only a lack of faith in the ability of his laymen, but also a lack of faith in the Holy Spirit who guides them.

Therefore, the first essential for a good adult program is a Committee on Adult Education meeting under the chairmanship of the rector. This book and other resources will enable such a committee to plan months, if not a whole year, in advance. (The details of planning for each adult class to be organized should be in the hands of its own steering committee. How this committee operates, and suggestions as to possible program material are discussed later.)

Experience has shown that the most effective adult classes meet every week for the period agreed on, although there are highly successful classes that meet less frequently. Some classes meet every week from September to June; others meet for periods of from four to eight weeks. In some parishes the parents' class meets while children are in their classes. In others, adult classes are held on an evening during the week.

We have dealt previously with the philosophy of the short term class in adult education. (See Chapter Three.) This is the ideal in terms of adult participation, interest, and the meeting of adult needs whether the class meets periodically or on a year round basis. The short term principle does not, however, stop adults from meeting weekly throughout the year. Short term (three to six weeks) refers to a group's involvement with a given topic or theme. Once that theme has been dealt with, a new topic or theme may be engaged with another short term period planned for. The year's work, thus, may be projected on the basis of a series of short term learning experiences for those groups that want to meet weekly. The work of the Committee on Adult Education is vital in such planning and guidance.

Sunday morning classes ideally have fifty-minute sessions. Unfortunately, in many instances less time is allowed and the consequent effectiveness of the class is impaired. Weeknight classes usually have ninety minutes, which is perhaps the most desirable length of time.

The size of classes also varies greatly. Tiny classes of

six or eight people meet in someone's home, in the choir stalls, or in a corner of the parish house auditorium. Neighborhood classes of eighteen to twenty-five people rotate their meetings from home to home or meet at the centrally located parish house on a weeknight when a room of ideal size is available. While good-sized classes of thirty to forty frequently have a room to themselves, they must meet sometimes in part of an auditorium while half a dozen children's classes drone away and scrape chairs in other parts of the room. Large classes of fifty or more, some even as large as two hundred, meet regularly in the church building and are still able to involve effectively a large proportion of those who attend.

Classes of almost every size, meeting in all kinds of circumstances, good and bad, have been tried. In subsequent chapters suggestions are made which should help any parish do the most effective job under its own particular circumstances. Chapter Six deals with the decisions the Committee on Adult Education will have to make which will affect directly the type of program possible. In the same chapter, the steering committee is also discussed—its task, its responsibilities, its method of operation. Chapter Seven treats teaching methods and techniques. Chapter Eight contains detailed suggestions on program.

Planning for Adult Education Classes

When a rector and parish Committee on Adult Education have decided to initiate a class for adults, they have a series of related matters to deal with before they can recruit a steering committee and charge its members with the responsibility of running the class. For purposes of illustration, here is an imaginary history of how one rector and his Education Committee worked.

For a long time the rector had thought his parish should have adult classes of some sort. However, it was not until the parish decided to use denominationally prepared church school courses that he was able to get enthusiastic support. In the late winter the rector and his newly organized Adult Education Committee decided to launch an adult class during the next fall. They also decided that the class should be open to any adult who wanted to attend, but that a special effort should be made to recruit the parents of children who were going to be in the three classes using the new courses.

Directly after Easter. the committee initiated a series of neighborhood meetings to inform parents about the proposed class. The rector and one or two members of the Education Committee sat down with groups of parents who had been invited by telephone to meetings in nearby parishioners' homes. The leaders told the twelve to fifteen parents present in each group something about the courses their children would be taking. They also explained the importance of adult Christian education in general and its particular importance for parents, especially the parents of children taking the new courses. The parents discussed the proposed class, asked questions, and, finally, most of them registered in advance. The rector and his fellow committeemen had decided previously that while they met with their neighborhood groups they would be on the lookout for people who might make good members of a steering committee.

The next step was to give the project general publicity. An announcement was made through the Sunday bulletin, backed up by some "talking around" by the clergy and the Adult Education Committee. The point was made that while the proposed class should include parents, and especially those whose children would be taking the new courses, there was no intention of excluding other adults. The matters which were to be discussed were relevant to the lives of all, whether they had children or not. As a result, there was a wave of additional advance registrations which brought the total number to sixty before the first of June.

The Education Committee had an emergency meeting. Some sort of "crash" program was going to be necessary. They had not expected such enthusiasm for the class.

A telephone survey of the registrants revealed that forty of them preferred to meet on Sunday morning. Most of the forty said they would not be able to attend a regular evening class. Twenty-three others preferred an evening meeting on some day other than Sunday. On the basis of this information, the committee decided to have two classes. The Sunday morning class would meet every week for fifty minutes during the time church school classes were in session. The tentative plan was for the other class to meet on Wednesday evenings for four separate series—six weeks or more in the fall, four to eight weeks in Epiphany, six weeks in Lent, and at least four weeks during the Easter season. The steering committee would have to decide exactly how long each series of sessions would be. This class would have ninety minutes per session.

Members for two steering committees were selected. The rector agreed to act as convener of both committees and scheduled his first meeting with them for early July.

This kind of preplanning was absolutely essential. As the Sunday morning steering committee analyzed its task, it discovered that it had special problems related to the length of the session and the fact that the class would have to meet in whatever space was not being used by church school classes. It might be the nave of the church, one end of the auditorium in which there were several children's classes, or even the large living room of a parishioner across the street. These difficulties did not deter them from having a class, however. They only meant that certain types of programs would not work effectively. It would be a part of the job of the committee to select procedures and techniques which would work in this particular situation.

The Wednesday evening steering committee had the advantage of a ninety minute session. There was also the advantage of being able to select the room in the parish house which suited their needs best. However, this group would probably have more difficulty with continuity of attendance than the Sunday group because it is not always easy for people—particularly parents—to arrange to attend a regular evening meeting. The committee would also have a recruiting job to do before each series started, and the composition of the group might change considerably from series to series. These factors would have to be taken into consideration as programs were planned.

This is the way one rector and his Adult Education Committee might have recruited and planned for an adult class. Early spring is a desirable time for planning a class scheduled to meet the following fall. The planning should include systematic recruiting of class members, careful selection of steering committee members, and a well-thought-out way to get the steering committee organized and started in its work.

Each class will, of course, need its own steering committee. Each steering committee will discover that the meeting time it has picked or been assigned will have certain advantages as well as drawbacks. Likewise, the room in which the class will have to meet will have certain limitations. These physical considerations will influence the kind of program presentation possible and in some cases the nature of the program itself. The committee will need to learn which of many teaching techniques and group procedures will work best under its particular circumstances.

6. THE ADULT EDUCATION COMMITTEE: PRELIMINARY PLANNING

THIS CHAPTER is addressed to each member of the steering committee as well as to the committee as a whole.

The purpose of an adult class is to provide an opportunity for every member to enter into a process through which he may discover the relevance of the Christian faith to his own life and daily relationships. Since this is a process of discovery rather than of accumulating information, your primary function is to guide or steer your class as it launches out into the deep waters of faith. You are not serving as experts who can answer all questions or give scintillating lectures, but rather as seekers who are willing to lend support and help to others who wish to join in this quest with you.

Your leadership is not that of an appointed position which carries authority and puts you in control of the group. You do not determine what this group should "learn," driving or steering it toward *your* purpose. Your leadership is to provide needed services. Thus, you make it possible for each member to make his contribution to the life of the group. In the development and deepening of this life together, the members can identify and discuss some of the issues of life and discover, through the power of the Holy Spirit working among you, how the Gospel speaks to issues under consideration. Your concern is primarily with people.

Your task can best be described in terms of its three most basic functions: listening, analyzing, and planning. There is no order of importance in these three functions. They must all be carried on simultaneously and continuously. Although in actual practice it is impossible to draw a clear line between them, the three functions are separated here for the purposes of study and examination.

If you are to help your class explore *its* concerns and not force it to deal with *your* concerns, you must listen to what the members are saying. You must know not only what was said but how it was said. What happened to the people in the class while the meeting was in progress? The recorder[1] will supply much of the information about what was said because it is his responsibility to record conclusions reached and questions asked, answered, or left unanswered. He will also capture some of the side remarks and comments not recorded on the newsprint or blackboard. The process observer[1] will note much of what happened. He can tell if the class worked together as a whole or if some people were left out. He will know whether or not the members built on the contributions made, and whether they were really interested in the subject or were just trying to do what they felt they were supposed to do. He can also tell much about the effect of the chairman on the group.

Here is a list of books which should be part of the working library of every steering committee. With one exception they are paper bound, inexpensive booklets. The total cost for all is reasonable. The steering committee of every class needs these inexpensive tools in order to do its job well.

Bergevin, Paul, et al., *Adult Education Procedures: A Handbook of Tested Patterns for Effective Participation*. New York: The Seabury Press, 1963. (paper)

---

1. The roles of *recorder* and *process observer* are fully explained in Strauss, *New Ways to Better Meetings*. (See listing.)

Bergevin, Paul and Dwight Morris, *A Manual for Discussion Participants.* New York: The Seabury Press, 1965. (paper)
Strauss, Bert, and Frances, *New Ways to Better Teaching.* New York: The Viking Press, 1964, revised edition.

The information presented by the recorder and the observer is of little use unless it is analyzed by the members of the steering committee. The recorder can tell what was said and the observer what happened, but the whole committee, working together with this information and against the background of what everyone heard and saw, must decide what all of this information means. Here are the kinds of questions you need to consider: If the class got bogged down in its last session was it because the members did not understand what they were doing? Was it because they lacked the necessary information to deal with the questions? Did the questions reflect the interest of the steering committee and not of the class? Dealing with such questions as these is the analyzing phase of your work and is vital to its effectiveness.

Thorough analysis will give you a good idea of where the class is and what is the real problem with which it is confronted. The next question is then, "How can we deal with this problem?" "Where do we go from here?" This is the planning phase of your work.

The term *planning* is frequently used in this book, but never forget that all plans made by the steering committee for class sessions must be regarded by the committee as suggestions only until they have been heard and accepted by the members of the class. When you make a suggestion you must listen to the reaction of the class. To force on these people a plan which they do not understand and accept is to begin "driving" rather than leading. Instead of performing a valuable service for them, you would then be making them perform for you. The other side of this coin is that the class may accept passively all plans you suggest. Then they are not doing their share of the work, but, instead, are forcing you into the position of dominance you are trying to avoid. If this happens you will have to help the class members make their own suggestions instead of depending upon you.

Does it seem that you are being asked to do an impossible job? It would be impossible for one person alone. No individual could provide all of the functions necessary to keep a class of this kind going and to help the members grow individually and collectively. Inevitably, an individual leader will dominate a group in one way or another. Fortunately, you are not expected to do this job alone. You are asked to be a member of a leadership group, the steering committee. The combined eyes, ears, and minds of this group can do what an individual alone cannot do.

Your pastor is your primary resource and support. Without his active help and support your task would be very difficult unless you have had a great deal of training and experience in this type of operation. He should not dominate the sessions of the class nor of the steering committee, but he can help you across many of the rough places you will encounter. To do this he must be aware of what you are planning and of the progress of the class. He will be willing to enter the class sessions as a resource person, but he should not lead the class sessions or sessions of the steering committee. In general, it is better if a clergyman does not even attend meetings of the class unless he is called in for a special task. However, particularly during the early part of the year, he should be urged to attend the weekly meetings of your steering committee. As you gain experience and as plans are laid out, he may attend steering committee meetings less frequently, although his support will always be needed.

Both the pastor and members of the steering committee should be familiar with the material in Chapter Eight: Planning Programs with Church Groups. It covers such topics as finding out which people are interested in studying, publicizing adult courses, and selecting suitable subjects.

Preclass Meetings

Your committee has considerable work to do before meeting with the class for the first time. This preparation is necessary if you are to build supporting relationships within the committee and to provide a common background of experience. Whether or not you can face your class with confidence the first time and get the year's work off to a good start will depend upon the thoroughness with which you do this work.

Experience indicates you will need about eight preclass meetings. These do not have to be held during consecutive weeks but can be arranged any way you wish. Three or four meetings might be held early in the summer and the rest concentrated in a few weeks before the class begins. Choose whatever schedule you wish, but do this work as thoroughly as possible.

If most or all members of the committee can attend a conference, preferably before the actual sessions of the class begin and preferably outside the parish house, it will mean a great deal to you and to the effectiveness of your operation.

The following is a suggested procedure to follow at the first meeting of the steering committee. Give each member a large name tag. Even if the group has only six or eight members, do not assume that committee members know one another. Begin the meeting with a discussion of the following questions: What is the purpose of the class we are about to guide? What is our task? How do we move from here?

The answer you decide upon to the question, "What is our task?" should be clearly and briefly stated on newsprint or a blackboard. Obviously, each steering committee should work out its own statement of its task.

The answer to the question, "How do we move from here?" may point to two needs which members of the committee have. You have to learn the leadership skills which will enable you to guide the class in its study and discussions and you have to become thoroughly familiar with the material you plan to use as content resource. After doing this you can make plans for the year.

The study of leadership comes first. Select a chairman, a recorder, and an observer. You might start by discussing the leadership task of your committee as it is described in this guide. This should be continued long enough to answer any questions committee members have, because everyone needs to gain an understanding of the kind of leadership the committee is expected to provide.

Then, move on to discuss the functions of the chairman, observer, and recorder. Read the description of these leadership functions in the group process books listed above. Remember, these are not mechanical offices with tightly defined duties; they represent skills that are resources to the group. Skills are developed by practice. Few people can step into one of these functions immediately, but nearly everyone can become proficient through practice and with the help of a sympathetic and friendly group.

An hour and a half is a good length of time for your meetings. The chairman should watch the schedule and call for the report of the observer while there is ample time to discuss it. About fifteen minutes should be sufficient for the report and a discussion of it at the close of the first few meetings. As time goes on, however, you may well spend up to thirty minutes discussing the report. A full discussion of the observer's report by your committee is of vital importance for your increasing understanding of what you are saying to and about each other and about yourselves in your meetings.

Content and Process

As you become familiar with the kind of leadership a steering committee is expected to provide, you will need also to become aware of the two languages in which every group converses. One is the language of words, called content. The other is the language of relationships, as expressed by attitudes and actions, and is called process. You will need to devote some of your preclass planning sessions to this subject in order to understand it fully.

Here is an illustration of the relation and importance of these two languages. A group is discussing the great value that Christianity places on the individual. The words they use say that Christians place great value on all people as individuals and children of God and that all people are important in the eyes of God. This is the content of their discussion. It may happen that during the progress of their discussion they do not listen well enough to hear fully what each person is saying and to build on suggestions and ideas expressed. Rather, it may be that each individual pushes his own point of view with little regard for what others have said, those speaking being interrupted by others seeking to be heard. In that case, the actions of the group say that the members do not really place much value on the individual. The language of their relationships contradicts the language of their words. Their process is saying the opposite of their content.

In Christian education the objective is for the individual to begin to discover the reality of the content of Christian teaching—as found in the Bible—as a true description of his life. Thus, for example, a person may know the words of the doctrine of original sin without having any feeling that this is a real description of the condition of his life. When he sees and feels the power and effect of sin in his own life, he has discovered the reality of the content of Christian teaching and immediately cries out for a Savior. Again, you may think that God loves you, but until you begin to experience the manifestation of this love it will never be a power in your life. The fact is that religion is far more concerned with knowing God and neighbor than with knowing about them.

The proper relation between content and process in Christian education is that the content describes and deepens what has already been experienced in process. Until content does this, we have only meaningless words. To be more specific, it has been said that we do not learn by experience but by reflecting upon or analyzing experience. As you relate to each other in the class (process), it is important that from time to time you analyze together what is actually going on. This analysis is the *content* describing the process of your experience. By comparing it with the *content* of Christian teaching, you may discover an explanation of what happened and why it happened. As you begin to see the deeper meaning of your own experience, real religious learning will take place.

You may all feel a bit uneasy when you first consider this matter of process. No one is anxious to have the implications of his actions discussed by a group. This sounds as if the group will sit in judgment on him and that he may be found unworthy by the group. If a study of process is ever allowed to become negative criticism of a person, then both the content and process are wrong. No person wants to relate negatively to other people, yet in varying degrees we all do. Your experience in the steering committee meetings and the experience which the class can provide are God-given opportunities, within the redemptive fellowship of the Church, to have a real relationship with a group of people who, in love, will be honest enough to tell you how you relate to others and still not reject you from their midst even if you offend. Where else could you have such an opportunity?

At first the process reports given by the observers will be on a rather superficial level. They may be discussed on the same level. As observers gain in skill, and as the group strengthens the supportive relationships among its members, the reports and the discussion of them will become more revealing and more helpful.

Before the end of each steering committee meeting, a chairman, a recorder, and an observer should be selected and plans made for the next meeting. By rotation, each member of the steering committee should have the opportunity to perform each of these functions at least once before the class begins.

Considering Techniques

The steering committee needs to become well versed in the techniques of group operation. The books listed on page 59 describe these techniques. Chapter Seven of this book is a discussion of the conditions under which the more commonly used techniques are appropriately employed. Note carefully the conditions as well as the use and purpose for which each is intended. Study the mechanical operation of each technique and practice various ones among yourselves in the committee.

During your preclass meetings, develop the technique of putting things on the blackboard or on sheets of newsprint hung on the wall by means of masking tape. (Brown paper masking tape is good for this purpose because it will adhere to almost any surface and will not damage most paint if it is not left in place more than twenty-four hours.) Points under discussion, points made during discussion, questions asked, and decisions reached should all be put on the board during the course of a discussion.

It helps a group to see before them such things as the questions given to discussion groups, the instructions as to the length of time, what the group is to do, and plans for next week. This is an important visual aid technique that will help keep your group clear on what is going on or what is to happen.

Newsprint sheets have an advantage over a blackboard in that they can be taken down at the end of the session and saved for the use of the steering committee or for the use of the whole class during the next session or some later session. Newsprint sheets are available from stationery stores or school supply stores. Many newspaper offices will sell or give you the ends of newspaper rolls that are too short to go through the press. If newsprint is difficult to obtain, try brown wrapping paper or shelf lining paper.

Remember that any one of these techniques is to be used only to help the class do its work. They are not to be used as "gimmicks" by which you manipulate the class to arrive at a goal chosen by the steering committee. The best and most interesting technique in the world is a failure if it does not help a group move to a deeper and clearer understanding of the question before it.

The First Session

After the general plans have been made, the first session of the class can be planned. Since we are all greatly influenced by first impressions, plans for the initial session of the class need to be given especially careful attention.

Be sure that all of your advanced planning is complete in detail. See that the place where the class meets is set up for the meeting. If not more than twenty-five are expected and space permits, arrange the chairs in a circle. If the group is larger, and space permits, arrange the chairs in small circles of five to eight. Be sure that newsprint and heavy black crayon or blackboard eraser and chalk are on hand. Have name tags near the door and have several crayons available so that more than one person can make a name tag at once. If you don't have self-stick tags, supply plenty of pins. Have several registration sheets available so that the class will not be unduly delayed by each individual having to sign a single sheet. See that the room is well lighted, ventilated, and at the proper temperature. Each member of the steering committee should be sure he understands his responsibility and is prepared to carry it out without delay or confusion.

Your procedure for the first meeting begins as the members of the class enter the room. Members of the steering committee should be on hand to guide people to the room and to greet them as they enter, then to assist them in making a name tag, signing the registration sheet, and finding a chair. All this should be done as quickly and with as little confusion as possible. If the rector is available, have him begin this first class session with a word of greeting and a statement of the importance of what the members are doing. He should then introduce the chairman for the day. The chairman will introduce the members of the steering committee and tell a little about its function. If it is not possible for the rector to be present in the class session, ask him to write a letter to members of the class stating his views on the importance of their work and his hopes for the class. In that case the meeting would be opened by the chairman with a word of greeting followed by the reading of the letter from the rector. Above all, make the beginning of this class seem important. Set an informal, warm, and friendly atmosphere, but do not waste time.

If the membership of the group is between forty and sixty, here is a procedure that has worked in some places. Immediately following the introductory remarks, divide the class into smaller sections of six to twelve people each, if this has not already been done. After members of the class are located in their small groups, explain to them that these are their discussion or work groups and that they will be working with this small group for the duration of the course. Get a list of each person in the group. Give these groups fifteen to twenty minutes to get acquainted with each other. Adopt whatever method of introduction seems feasible to you, and have the introductions made within the small groups rather than to the total group.

The remainder of the session can be used to explain to the class something of the possible plans of action that might be taken during the coming weeks. Emphasize that group members will have a share in deciding what is done and that no decision will be made immediately. Ask them to think about the suggestions during the coming week and to be prepared to enter into a decision the following session.

The general impression that members of the class get of this first session is important. Plan carefully so that everything will move smoothly, promptly, and purposefully. Be warm and supporting in your relations with the group, and above all do your best to create an atmosphere of expectation looking toward the rest of the year.

If your group numbers more than sixty, try to make arrangements to divide it into more than one class. Classes of from thirty to fifty achieve a higher level of involvement and participation. Frequently, because it is not possible to divide into smaller groups, a class as large as a hundred or more has to meet as a unit. Under such circumstances the members can still be involved in discussion and there can be a degree of participation, but it will not be as great as in small classes. In any case, note carefully the recommendations on pages **73** to **87** as to which techniques work best in small groups and in large.

The Steering Committee: Guiding the Class

One of the first problems you are likely to encounter is the lack of continuity in attendance of the members of the class. Of those present one week, some will be absent the next week, and new people may join. This is a problem common to all adult classes, and no surefire cure has been found. However, here are some suggestions that may help.

If the class can be divided into permanent groups of eight, as suggested, keeping track of absentees is comparatively easy. Post on the wall a list of the small groups so that every person will remember where he belongs and who the members of his group are.

There are some questions about subdividing which your committee should consider in advance, however. For example, should husbands and wives be in the same group? How should members of the steering committee distribute themselves throughout the groups and what role should each play in his or her group?

It has been suggested that at the beginning of every

session of the class a recorder for each group give a brief report as to how many are present and what has happened to the absentees in his group. Groups should be encouraged to get in touch with absent members before the next session. This will help people feel they are missed when they do not attend and having a small group to tie to will give them some real reason for coming. The impersonal feeling of "just being a member" of a large group may have some relation to the problem of steady attendance.

Should a group be reduced for any one session to fewer than five members, assign those present to other groups for that session. If the size of a group is seriously reduced by withdrawals from the class, consolidate it with the other groups and make new lists showing the permanent members of the remaining groups. Do not *ever* leave people isolated in a group too small to be effective or too small to make its members feel equal to the rest of the groups. You may well have to reassign your groups after the class has been operating for a month or six weeks. Many who are enthusiastic at first may drop out if the class goes on indefinitely. New members should be assigned to groups immediately. If the groups begin to go above eight members, redivide the class and create new groups. Visitors are assigned to groups to fill in for absent members.

The members of the steering committee should study the list of names of those who have attended and be prepared to greet people and address them by name during the sessions. This is a good way to show through "process" that you are interested in those who attend.

If the class is a large one of seventy-five or more, a telephone to get in touch with absentees can do a great deal toward helping to maintain a high level of regular attendance. No matter what size the class, watch the degree of involvement of individual members of the class. Individuals who are not involved or who look bored are likely to be susceptible to temptations to be absent. The observer or one of the members of the steering committee should have the responsibility of noting these symptoms, which grow so easily into spasmodic attendance. When your steering committee is working on ways in which to increase group involvement, its members are also using one of the best possible methods to preserve continuity of attendance.

Reaction Blanks

The use of reaction blanks or opinion sheets, such as the one illustrated on page 71, is a valuable aid to the steering committee and a help to the class. If possible, allow time near the end of each session for members of the class to fill out the reaction blank. You cannot tell much about the reaction of the class until you have used such a blank several times. Some groups are habitually conservative in their rating of sessions whereas others are enthusiastic and generous in their ratings.

You will have to find the average for your group before you can differentiate accurately between an effective and an ineffective session. You will also need experience in interpreting the remarks of class members as well as their scale ratings. Some people will say they do not like a certain session when, in reality, while they found it unpleasant and disturbing, they found it extremely valuable. Be sure you explain to the class the purpose of the blank before asking that it be filled out. In your explanation, stress the necessity for honest reaction on the part of members of the class and make it clear that they are not expected to sign their names.

It is a good idea to let the class know that members of the steering committee read these blanks and pay attention to them. One way to do this is to post a graph of the reactions of the group to each session. This can be done by posting the average numerical rating those present gave the session. If a graph of these averages is made and posted on the wall of the room where the class meets, class members can see their reactions to each session visualized.

You might also, each week, post in summary form some of the significant comments or reactions turned in so that group members have an evaluation of their own reactions to the previous session. From time to time, you may find items on the blanks that will be profitable to discuss for your own clarification or for the enlightenment of the group. Whenever the blanks have a strong influence on the planning of a session, let the class know this.

Some groups dislike opinion blanks. If you meet resistance on the part of the class, it is wise to discontinue their use for a while. However, this resistance usually comes because the group feels no real use is made of the opinion blanks. If they see that they are used in guiding the progress of the class, most groups are more than willing to fill them out.

Opinion Blank

1. How well do you think we worked together today? (Rate your feelings on the line below. A rating of 1 means "not at all"; 5 means "extremely well.")

1	2	3	4	5

2. What would have caused you to rate the session higher (if you rated it lower than 5)?
3. How interesting do you think the discussion was?

completely uninteresting	rather uninteresting	so-so	very interesting	extremely interesting

4. Why did you rate the above as you did?
5. Comments and suggestions.

Help the members of your group understand that you do not anticipate a detailed reaction under each heading of the opinion blank, but that you would like the blanks to reflect briefly and honestly the dominant reactions of the class to the session. It shouldn't take more than two or three minutes for anyone to fill out a blank.

Planning Week by Week

The steering committee must meet weekly to evaluate the previous class session and to plan for the next session. Don't depend upon the general impressions of the members of the committee as to what happened in the last session; instead, use all the definite information you have. The reaction blanks turned in by members and the reports of the observer and the recorder are excellent sources of information about what happened. These three sources can, of course, be combined with the impressions gained by members of the steering committee. Then, consider what this information says about last week's session. If the session was not effective, why wasn't it? If it was effective, what were its good points? In the light of what happened in the last class, you can determine where the class is and the direction in which it is going. Next, determine what resources and techniques will best forward this process in the next session of the class.

Remember, simplicity helps to avoid confusion. Choose only the techniques and resources that are necessary to advance the work of a session. If one technique will accomplish the task, don't use two. If the class has sufficient information to take the next step, don't add more information which may be confusing rather than helpful.

Use variety in your techniques and methods of presentation. A new technique or an old one that has not been used for a long time can do a great deal to add life to a session.

Above all, avoid falling into the habit of using a pat technique or method again and again. Use your imagination and ingenuity freely but wisely.

Changing Course

Steering committees sometimes feel that once they have made a commitment to study a certain course or have adopted a certain book around which to center their program, they must hew to the line and, automatically, exclude other sources. This need not be the case and sometimes *should* not be. Your object is to guide your class in a series of learning sessions in which all of you together discover new vistas of meaning for your lives, individually and as a group, in the Christian good news. There is no virtue in following doggedly through a study of material (even the Bible) merely for the sake of covering that material. This could be the wrong year, or the wrong group, or the wrong steering committee to work on a certain subject and you may not discover it until the class has been meeting for weeks. If that should happen, don't feel discouraged. It has happened before. Consult with your rector, and make a fresh start. No apologies are needed and the rest of the year is likely to go well because you have learned a certain freedom within the discipline of your task.

Some classes fall in love with an unbalanced diet. They are so enthralled with the exploration of life's basic questions that they forget and ignore the vast body of Christian heritage about which they should also be informed. If the class bogs down, it may be that a solid lecture on Christian doctrine, group Bible study, or a conducted meditation, may be just what is needed.

The opposite situation may also be true. A class may have been too timid to come to grips with the relevance of the Christian faith for their lives and have spent weeks and weeks in objective consideration of a Christian belief or a portion of the Bible. Your committee may need to face the fact that you should be leading the class away from an objective study of classical Christion beliefs into a consideration of the problems of daily life and relationships, and the light the Gospel throws on them.

From time to time, every steering committee ought to take stock of itself and its work in order to be certain it is performing the task for which it was organized.

7. METHODS AND TECHNIQUES

As was said earlier, the art of being able to involve members of a class so that they become active participants will go a long way toward solving the problem of spasmodic attendance. It is also closely related to learning. The more a person is involved, the more he participates in the life and discussion of a class, the more he learns. Participation involves more than is ordinarily supposed. The fully-responsible participant does more than say something during a discussion or ask a question when the opportunity is given.

The steering committee needs to give careful attention to the way members of the class participate. Closely related, of course, is the kind of leadership the committee will need to espouse and encourage in order to stimulate a high level of member participation. There are several helpful, yet brief, treatments of the nature of a good discussion, the role of the leader, and the responsibilities of participants. One of these is *A Manual for Discussion Participants* by Paul E. Bergevin and Dwight Morris. This book is part of the working library recommended for every steering committee. The effectiveness of your committee's work will materially improve if you study it thoroughly during preliminary planning sessions and refer back to it for review several times during the year. The art of conducting and participating in a good discussion is fundamental to any serious work done by people in groups. The techniques suggested in the following section will be of much greater value to the class if committee members are continually working at the task of improving their ability, and that of members of the class, in the art of group discussion.

Techniques

Techniques are used to involve as many members of a class as possible in consideration of the issue at hand. The extent to which techniques are wisely selected and wisely used is likely to be in direct proportion to the amount of learning which takes place.

The successful operation of any group technique depends in large measure upon the clarity of the instructions given. Be sure that each person thoroughly understands what he is doing and how long he has to do it. For example, questions given to discussion groups should be clearly stated, and the entire group should understand how long they have for discussion. After the committee has given the group an explanation of the technique to be employed and has given detailed instructions to each person involved or to each group involved, provide opportunity for questions so that any misunderstandings can be clarified before discussion begins.

Here are three questions regarding techniques which must be faced in planning a session:

What technique shall we use?

Why will we be using it?

How do we do it?

The following discussion takes up the particular uses of certain techniques and the limitations to be considered because of the size of the class and/or the nature of the physical surroundings. For the details of "how to do it," reference is made to manuals and pamphlets in the steering committee working library. There are also a few references to materials which should be part of every parish library. (See the Bibliography.)

Small Group Discussion

Small group discussions are sometimes referred to as "huddles" or "buzz groups." No matter what they are called, the idea refers to a procedure which puts the members of a class into groups of five to eight people to discuss a specific, provocative question.

This technique may be used at the beginning of a session to warm up to a new subject. It may be used in the course of a session to involve the members in the subject under consideration. After an initial presentation by a speaker or a panel, for example, the class can divide into small groups to discuss specific questions. Thus everyone is involved actively in a consideration of the subject.

Sometimes, small groups are used for clarification. When it has become evident from the general discussion or questions from the floor that members of the class are hazy about the issues involved, it is often helpful to divide into small groups to consider a carefully worded question designed to help everyone get a clear grasp of the subject.

Another use for this technique is to broaden the discussion by gaining other points of view. Suppose a panel has just discussed a controversial subject and, as a result, several views of it have been listed on the blackboard. The leader knows that there are other points of view about the subject and he suspects that several of them are smoldering in the minds of members of the class. The use of small groups can bring them out in the open and give the class an opportunity to consider the subject more fully and more fairly.

It is now obvious that a chief reason for using small group discussion is to enable more people to express themselves. In the class as a whole many voices will be heard, but there are always quiet members who will not make the effort to speak out, especially when the floor is being monopolized by a talkative minority. In small groups, however, the contributions of quieter class members are needed, sought, and heard. Something else happens to people who are put into the same small discussion groups on successive occasions—they get to know each other intimately. They come to understand and appreciate why it is that the others think and feel as they do. An important reason for assigning permanent membership in small groups, then, is because people working together over a period of time develop a high degree of respect, acceptance, and rapport.

Small discussion groups may be used effectively in any size group. A group of eight is already a good size for discussion purposes; a group of nine to fifteen can be divided into two. There have been occasions on which as many as one thousand people have been put into small discussion groups. This technique can be used successfully at a meeting in the nave of the church. It is, of course, easier to use in a room which has movable chairs, and is still more ideal when each smaller group can have its own room. This latter procedure, however, often consumes precious time in the going and coming.

It is difficult for groups to report verbally back to the chairman if another part of the room is being used by other classes. Under such circumstances, small discussion groups have to work as quietly as possible and report back in writing.

Role-Playing

Role-playing is the unrehearsed, spontaneous acting out of a problem in relationships. Situation-oriented, it is a good way to illustrate or introduce such a problem. When a situation is acted out before them, members of a class can *see* the problem to which they are addressing themselves. Role-playing is also a good way to test the validity of a solution. For example, suppose an adult class is considering the Christian implications of schoolroom discipline. It has been decided that the best way for a teacher to deal with a particularly obstreperous child is to make him stand out in the hall. By acting out the situation as a role-play group members will be able to see what effect this action will have on the rest of the child's class while the child being disciplined is in the hall and what will happen to the class when he is allowed to return.

Still another reason for using role-play is to show members of a class the effect their behavior has on others. Suppose a class has discussed rejection but does not consider it a serious problem. The steering committee might plan to start the next session with a role-play which would reveal that class members are frequently insensitive to the extent to which they reject others and also insensitive to what rejection does to people. A further value of this technique is that the role-player himself is sometimes helped to appreciate the feelings of someone in a situation in which he has never yet found himself.

It is easy to see that role-playing is an effective way of holding up before a class the situation or the concept being discussed. It is used to let people test realistically their answers and conclusions. It enables members of a class to see and study behavior which is frequently their own. It is also a way to introduce a fundamental problem without providing a solution. And it is an excellent way to help people improve their ability to observe process—what is really happening between class members in contrast to what is being discussed.

The use of role-playing is limited to situations in which all the members of the class can see and hear. It is not likely to be effective in a very large group or when a class has to share an auditorium with other classes. However, multiple role-plays—a number of role-plays going on simultaneously in small groups—make it possible to use this technique under almost any circumstances.

The use of role-play as a method requires a certain degree of skill and understanding upon the part of the leader. The following guide lines are presented with the hope that the leader will comprehend the nature of his task, as well as be led to do considerable research and study before using this technique.

When setting up a role-play:

- choose only *one* situation to be role-played.
- choose a situation that is a real life situation, thus familiar to the participants.

- define the role-play situation, setting forth the points and/or counter points to be made.
- brief the spectators as to what they are to watch for, *etc.*
- cut the role-play when the point has been set forth. Do not press for a solution. Usually, short scenes are best, about five to seven minutes or less.
- question the characters regarding their feelings while playing the assigned roles. Also, question the audience regarding feelings, observations, and reactions.
- derole the players before returning them to the audience.
- allow discussion to flow from the role-play.

In using this method or technique, remember to:

- stop when the point is made.
- limit the play to ONE situation.
- use a typical problem, not a fantasy.
- use the play NOT TO SOLVE, but to clarify and state the problem.
- make certain not to cast people in their own life roles.
- avoid stereotyping a person in several roles.
- "release" or "derole" the actors from their roles quickly.
- Let the audience respond to the play.

Skits

Skits, like role-plays, are the unrehearsed acting out of problems in relationships. Unlike role-plays, they are not spontaneous but have been written out, and the parts are read by the participants. A skit is used as a means of preinvolvement, that is, to warm up a class to the subject for the day. It is also used when it is necessary to get across a particular point or set of ideas. The skit may present an exact statement of the problem, give definite answers through the words and actions of characters, or seek to communicate a point of view.

A skit is a technique of indoctrination. It is a way of being certain of what is said and even what is heard because the members of the class may be given copies and asked to look for certain things. A skit should not be used alone. It might be used to present specific methods and concepts, but it should be followed by, for example, small group discussions in order to be sure everyone understood what was said.

The same conditions which determine the effectiveness of role-plays apply to skits. All the members of the group must be able to see and hear. A skit, therefore, would not be very effective for a class which meets in the corner of a large auditorium in which other classes also are meeting.

Interviews

An interview as a group process technique is a means of acquainting a group with a visitor and his point of view on specific subjects. It is used as a method of introduction or as a way of carrying a class into consideration of a problem. An interview is likely to be most effective when it is followed by a question period, by general discussion, or by small group discussions to give members of the class an opportunity to explore the subject further.

The only limitation on the use of this technique is whether or not all present can see and hear, as in the case with role-playing or skits.

Lecture

A lecture is the presentation (usually uninterrupted) of a subject or a problem by one person. This is the most common way of giving a class factual information. It is one way to use a resource person who has been brought into the class. His presentation comes as an answer to the felt need of the class for more light on a problem, for a more comprehensive consideration of a subject than the members were able to make themselves.

Panel Discussion

A panel discussion is a procedure in which several people engage in a staged but informal consideration of a subject in order to interest or enlighten a larger group. A panel is used as an initiating device—to arouse interest or to introduce the problem. It is also used to broaden a discussion by presenting different points of view or presenting experts who have the facts. It may be used also to summarize a discussion in an effort to present as a composite picture the facets of the problem and the possible solutions arrived at by smaller groups within the class.

Here again the technique is limited in its use principally by whether those present can see and hear. A panel, however, is primarily a technique for large groups. Other methods are likely to be more effective if the group has fewer than thirty members.

Group Bible Study

This is a technique by means of which a class is working as a whole and in small discussion groups seeks to understand a portion of the Bible. Group Bible study (see Chapter Nine) is one way to deepen insights or take a fresh look at the nature of issues with which a class is dealing. As members of the class gain a new understanding of a particular book or other portion of the Bible, they may come to appreciate the community of the Holy Spirit of whose heritage the Bible is a significant part. They may also come to see the relevance of the particular biblical material to their own lives and situations because in it they see the way in which God and man are related—a reflection of their own individual or corporate situations. The search for relevance must not be the primary goal of Bible study, however, or the temptation to moralize or to distort will become almost inescapable.

There is another caution related to Bible study: it may be nothing but flight from reality. A class could engage in a study of biblical concepts—the idea of covenant, faithfulness, Isaiah's idea of God—which would be purely academic. While such a study might be made interesting, it would have nothing to do with the lives of the people in the class. It would be a comfortable, sanctified way to escape from being confronted by the religious significance of one's life and relationships. At the same time, it is equally a misuse of Scripture to use the status of the Bible to bolster an already espoused point of view. The Bible is not to be used as a gimmick.

Group Bible study is possible for almost any size group.

Audio-Visual Resources

Audio-visual resources include such materials as films, filmstrips, and slides (with or without sound), posters, pictures, diagrams, and bulletin boards. These may be used to introduce a problem or subject for discussion. They may be used to bring information and new light on a subject. They may crystallize the insights gained by the class. It is most important for members of the committee to think through clearly *why* they want to use such materials. Audio-visual resources should never be used for entertainment. Their proper use in a class usually requires more work and planning on the part of the steering committee than any other technique.

The principal limitation in the use of films is availability. It is often difficult to get what you want when you want it. If there is a film library in your locality the film may already be booked on the date you want it. If you have to order it, you will need to know a long time in advance what film you want and on what date, and there is always the problem of whether the film will arrive in time for the meeting. Another difficulty is being able to get a desired film far enough in advance to preview it and a preview is a must. In spite of these problems, the right film at the right time, used in the proper way, is extremely effective and is a superb teaching technique.

The same difficulties do not apply to filmstrips, slides, flat pictures, and the like. A parish can own them and they can be used whenever necessary.

Other Techniques

There are other techniques which can be used in various combinations with those suggested above. Some of these (such as "brainstorming" and the open-ended story) are described in the books and pamphlets recommended as the steering committee's basic working library. The techniques discussed above are the procedures every steering committee should be prepared to use when they are most appropriate.

Don't Rush

Remember that you don't have to do everything in one session; a technique may profitably be spread over several. You can, for instance, give the class the background for a role-play in one session and have the small groups discuss the approach they are going to make in playing it out. The second session can be devoted to the role-play. If time permits, the groups may begin their evaluation of what happened. A third session could be used for the final evaluation of what happened in the role-play and for the presentation of group reports. Or the groups can simply present their reports and discuss them. Such a procedure, of course, assumes continuity of attendance; otherwise it will not work.

In initiating any procedure in a class session be careful that your instructions are clear and definite. Always ask for questions so that misunderstandings are cleared up before the procedure begins. Confusion in the class can generally be charged to the steering committee and not to members of the class. Wherever possible, mimeograph instructions and give them to each person involved in the procedure. These written instructions should always be discussed to be certain that they are clear.

Confusion can easily be mistaken for "flight" from the issue being discussed. (See below.) A group cannot discuss a subject profitably about which they have no definite convictions or about which they have insufficient information. Use resources to provide an adequate background for worthwhile discussion.

Awareness of What DID *Happen*

Every steering committee has a big job and a demanding one. Sometimes a class session may seem to be a failure and the cause is not apparent. The question under discussion may appear to be of interest to the class, but something happens. The techniques chosen have been used before, and successfully. This time they do not seem to get the desired results in interest, involvement, participation, and understanding. What's the matter?

Here are several considerations of which a steering committee needs to be aware. They have an influence on both the progress of class and the effectiveness of the techniques used.

Flight

Flight is the term used to describe the retreat of any group from live issues onto "safe" ground. Any group involved in facing a vital question on which there is real difference of opinion will, from time to time, resort to flight. If this is not recognized and handled wisely, it can impede the progress of the group and ultimately destroy the group itself. Members of a group will retreat from involvement in an issue if they are pushed too deeply into it too quickly, or if they take themselves too quickly into it too deeply. Sometimes the need to provide time to think something over will cause a group to leave an issue temporarily. When a group has been working well, fatigue can cause it to seek rest in flight. You will notice that often, after a particularly good session where much hard work was done, nothing much is done in the next session. The group wants to rest awhile before moving on.

Flight is characterized by the almost complete disappearance of genuine relevance. Everything seems to be in the realm of words. All discussion is on a superficial level. When a group stops discussing on a first person level and begins using such terms as *they* or *people* and discussing abstract ideas, it may be retreating from concrete reality into abstraction (although not every treatment of the abstract is a retreat from reality). Any sudden change in the direction of a discussion which takes it to another subject or issue may be evidence of flight.

Whenever your group resorts to flight, the steering committee should look first at itself in search of the cause. Was the group pushed too fast or too deep? If the discussion becomes too threatening, an individual will often protect himself by running away. If this seems to be the cause, then you must plan to involve the class more carefully to enable them to move along.

Another question you must ask is, "Was this flight or just confusion?" Did the group have sufficient information to do what it was asked to do, and did members understand what they were asked to and why they were asked to do it? If the class is confused, then you must supply the group with better instructions and test to see if they are understood clearly and if the group accepts the suggested task as important. Don't overlook the necessity of providing the resource of factual information unless you are reasonably certain this would only serve as an escape from facing the issue rather than furthering the life of the class.

Was the chairman leading or driving? Was he helping the group to deal with its concern or trying to force members to deal with *his* concern? These questions must also be faced by the steering committee in seeking to discover the cause of flight. If the answer is yes, then you must attempt to get back to the concerns of the class.

Every group will, from time to time, rest itself. A rest period may last for an entire class session. This is natural. It can be profitable and should be allowed. Only by experience can you determine if the class was just resting, was confused, or was in flight.

In general, the cure for flight is gentle, reassuring leadership plus the provision of the necessary tools to help the class overcome its difficulty and feel free to move forward again.

Sometimes it may be helpful for members of the class to consider why they were running away from reality, from facts, or from each other. Often this results in real learning. Why is the safety of flight more important to the members than the rewards of involvement? If the answer is judgmental, the judgment must fall on the entire class, for all are responsible if even some are seeking protection in flight.

On Exploring a Vital Subject

The primary purpose of exploring a vital, fundamental question is not to add to the store of information of class members but rather to help each member find the grace and power to live under the tension created by the issue, whatever it is. This involves a change in the life of the individual.

In personal terms, exploration of an issue (such as "whom [or what] do I really look to as my savior") depends upon the quality of the life of the class and the recognition by the members of their own involvement in it. Unless members of the class feel free in the presence of each other and of their leadership, they will tend to keep discussion on a theoretical level. The committee can help develop an atmosphere of freedom by its attitude toward the class. It should be careful to encourage those who make contributions rather than to pass judgment on them. All contributions to a discussion should be received even if they seem ridiculous and beside the point. The chairman should never say such things as, "That is wrong," or, "That is not what we are talking about." If a person makes a statement that seems to be off the point, he should be asked to expand it. Often when he does it will be found that the first statement was a poor expression of a good idea.

Committee members should be quick to protect individuals from ridicule by other members of the group. If a member makes a statement and several other members laugh at it, he should be defended by suggesting that the class think about his point before deciding it is wrong. If the leadership is warm and accepting rather than judgmental, this attitude will gradually spread through the class.

To be willing to work on a truly touchy question, the individual must recognize that it deals with a problem which is important to him. The chairman cannot explain this; it must be discovered. Exploration, then, must begin with people where they are and gradually lead them, step by step, deeper into the issue.

In the early stages of exploring an issue, the discussion may well be carried on in impersonal terms. Hypothetical cases or general principles may be used as a means of getting started. In guiding a class into the discussion of an issue, the leader should be very sensitive to the class's reaction. The class will generally move as rapidly as the members are able to move and as rapidly as the resources which are provided help them to move.

As an illustration of this, here are some steps by which a class might move into the exploration of some of the tensions that develop between parents and children. The process could begin with a case history illustrating some of the "terrible" things children do. This could lead to the discussion of the failure of some parents. From such a discussion the class might move on to a further discussion of how parents can prevent their children from doing such things. Next, to go even deeper, the class would have a role-play involving the question, "What would you do if your child did such and such a thing?" From this role-play, the class could move into a second role-play involving the question, "If you were the child, how would you feel if your parents acted this way toward you?" Afterward, the class could discuss the question, "How can I, as a sinful person relate to my child in such a way that he may experience the grace and power of God in his life?" Working through this question can bring out the deeper question, "How can I find the power of God in my life so that my children will see it reflected in me?" If the last question were asked first, the group would, in all probability, immediately back away from any consideration of its real meaning.

The Danger of Success

If the steering committee works at its preclass training sessions, and if, as the year goes on, its members meet weekly to evaluate each session held and to plan the next session, experiencing together the trials and triumphs of the work, there will develop inevitably a strong cohesive spirit within the group. This spirit is good and is necessary for the effective operation of the class. It should be pointed out, however, that this strong spirit within the steering committee can become a threat to the effective operation of the class. Should the members of the class feel that the committee has become a special "group within a group" with a special relationship to the rector, committee members may find themselves isolated from the rest of the class.

This can be avoided if the committee is careful to use members of the class in every way possible and to include them in meetings of the steering committee. From time to time it is a good idea to invite one or two members of the class who are not on the steering committee to meet with it just to see the work that is done and to share in the planning. As the class grows in experience, members of the class may be asked to serve as chairman, observer, or recorder. When members of the class are asked to serve in these functions, they should be invited to attend the steering committee meeting prior to the session of the class when they will serve. They should also be invited to the next meeting of the steering committee to give their evaluation of what happened. The steering committee should always be particularly alert and sensitive to their suggestions and criticisms, as well as to those of other class members. If the class feels that the committee is genuinely serving their interests, rather than having a good time within its own group, then its work with the class and for the class will continue to be effective.

During class sessions, members of the steering committee must avoid the temptation to draw together in a group to watch members of the class work. Of course, the chairman for the day, the observer, and the recorder have their duties outlined for them. It is advisable for other members of the steering committee to fit into discussion groups as normally as possible. Steering committee members may be used to fill out a discussion group hard hit by absences, or they may be distributed among all the discussion groups. They do not enter the group as experts but just members of the group team. They should resist the temptation to dominate the group or to let the group force them into a position of special leadership.

Additional Resource Books

Bornkamm, Gunther, *The New Testament: A Guide to Its Writing.* Philadelphia: Fortress Press, 1973.

Minor, Harold, *Creative Procedures for Adult Groups.* Nashville: Abingdon Press, 1968.

———, *New Ways for a New Day.* Nashville: Abingdon Press, 1965.

Rendtorff, Rolf, *God's History: A Way Through the Old Testament.* Philadelphia: Westminster Press, 1969.

Wilckens, Ulrich, *God's Revelation: A Way Through the New Testament.* Philadelphia: Westminster Press, 1970.

Wolff, Hans W., *The Old Testament: A Guide to Its Writings.* Philadelphia: Fortress Press, 1973.

Bread, Bible Reading Fellowship, Box 299, Winter Park, Florida 32789.

8. PLANNING PROGRAMS WITH CHURCH GROUPS

MANY ADULTS have had some experience with program planning for clubs, church groups, or community organizations. Some people seem to have a knack for it; they are known for their interesting programs. They have energy, ideas, and organizational skill. However, even such "good" program chairmen have occasional failures. Why? Can this art be learned? Is it an individual or a group skill?

The reader who has planned programs in Christian education will readily agree that it is not a task for beginners. By the nature of this responsibility in the life of the Church, the leader is confronted with certain conditions necessary to equip him for the task. The usual characteristics of Christian leadership are equally demanded of the program planner. However, it is essential that the basic conditions be stated here because of their bearing on creative and effective program planning.

(1) Have an understanding of the nature and purpose of the Christian Church, in particular the role of the parish in accomplishing this purpose.

(2) Have an understanding and active sympathy with the idea of lay leadership in small groups. There are many good books and guides which bring the leader into contact with the studies and development of leadership and leadership styles.

(3) Be familiar with the content and recommended methods of study of the materials to be used. A parish will grow in the ability to plan programs and to meet the specific needs and interests of its own people when it has already used some of the reading and discussion courses available. These courses will serve to awaken interest in learning more about Christianity and will provide training both for leaders and group participants.

Why Good Program Planning Is Important

One of the major tasks of the Church is to teach the good news to its members and to help them express it in their daily living in a complex and changing world. The Church is not a man-made institution. It is a divine organism of clergy and people, with Christ as its head, founded by him to carry on his redemptive work in the world. *Because of its very nature, the Church speaks with authority in matters of religion and morals.*

One might, therefore, infer that all the Church needs to do in teaching the faith is to compel people to memorize a catechism of essential teachings and to give occasional authoritative lectures explaining them. Some parishes actually proceed on this basis. The results are usually highly unsatisfactory. In today's world it cannot be assumed that children grow up in a truly Christian family, even if the parents attend church, for the parents' understanding of the faith and its practice may be quite fragmentary and defective. All of us, adults and children alike, live in a society where secular and anti-Christian views are subtly and constantly presented to us. Against these long years of anti-Christian indoctrination, catechism and lectures are singularly ineffective in changing people's beliefs and their daily lives. Furthermore, it is widely recognized that the way of educating adults, even in secular matters, must be quite different from that of high school or college students. The latter are candidates for a degree, and if they want the degree they must complete the studies prescribed by the faculty and pass the examinations. Adults, however, are not compelled to study; they do it only if they wish to; therefore, they study only material that is of *interest* to them. The growth of the adult education movement in the secular world in the past quarter century is the result of offering a wide variety of courses that appeal to people's interests.

This presents a real dilemma: While the Church must teach, by divine command—and with authority—most adults will give of their spare time only to follow their own interests. Fortunately, this dilemma can be resolved without violating theology. The integrity of the person is important and the Church must try to win people of their own free will, rather than push them around. Even more important, it is a part of Christian belief that no man can force faith on another—this comes only as a gift of God the Holy Ghost. Freedom and authority must, therefore, exist side by side.

From this it follows that the role of leader in Christion education is somewhat like that of the farmer. It is God who makes the crops grow, but the farmer who plants the seed and helps by providing a favorable environment. The problem is actually much more complicated, for human beings are not passive plants. The provision for suitable spiritual and intellectual food and a favorable environment for spiritual growth remain of central importance. The Church still teaches with authority, but she is infinitely patient and willing to help people learn about any given subject matter and in a way that is interesting to them.

Because good program planning has to do with finding and meeting the needs of people, it should now be obvious why it is of importance in the Church's teaching. The following six steps cover the basic points that need to be considered in good program planning.

1. Finding Interests of Participants
2. Selecting the Topics
3. Defining Aims
4. Uncovering Resources
5. Choosing Effective Group Procedures
6. Outlining the Program in Detail

Step One: Finding Interests of Participants

The only sure way to get a good-sized group of adults to come to a meeting and to have them derive real benefit from it is to appeal to their interests. Offering people "something that is good for them"—that is, trying to meet their needs, or what somebody believes their needs to be, is not effective. People either stay away or, if they come, listen passively and go away unchanged.

The principle fault of ordinary church program planning is precisely this. A program chairman makes plans. If this individual is imaginative and his interests are typical of the group to be appealed to, his programs may be successful, but the odds are against it. How often we hear such an individual say, "I planned a good meeting but nobody came." He may have planned the meeting around *his* interests, or he may have tried to meet real needs that theology points out, but which the people did not recognize as their personal concern. It is for these reasons that good program planning is not a one-man operation. The participants must be involved, if not always directly, at least through a representative planning or steering committee. *People participate more actively in, and feel responsible for the success of a meeting when they have taken part in planning it.*

Some clergy may feel that the Church is abdicating her responsibility if meetings are planned to meet parishioners' *interests* rather than their *needs.* For example, a priest may feel that his people *need* to know more about the Church's teaching on Christian stewardship, or about the doctrine of judgment; most laymen, however, don't recognize these subjects as needs and wouldn't come to a meeting to learn about them. By using interests as a key, and by using a relaxed, informal atmosphere in which everyone is encouraged to think, to question, to read, and to speak out, the deeper needs of the participants will be discovered and worked on in a way that is significant to them. To carry out this type of program effectively, careful planning well in advance of the meeting is required. It cannot be improvised hastily at the last minute.

On the other hand, situations will arise occasionally where a distinguished visitor or a visiting missionary is found to be available. Usually, such persons make a speech that is followed by a few sporadic questions. Two things can be done to improve such a program. The easiest plan is to announce *before the speaker starts* that the audience is requested to ask questions at the end and distribute 3 x 5 cards for notetaking. More people will listen attentively and the discussion period will be better.

Another way to vary this program is to tell the audience in advance that they will be asked to divide afterward into huddles to talk over the lecture for a few minutes and to find questions for the speaker. A still better way is *to get the audience involved before the lecture starts* by having a committee or the chairman interview the speaker in advance and prepare four or five "discussion statements" or provocative questions on the subject of the lecture (written on the blackboard), and have the audience warm up by discussing them in groups of ten or twelve for ten or fifteen minutes before the lecture begins. They will then listen with greater interest, the question period at the end will be livelier, and more people will participate.

How to Find Interests

Good program planning is not an individual but a group task. A parish, or a group of adults who indicate a desire to study, finds great benefit in having a series of interest-finding sessions. This is most beneficial in the early stages of group life. The individual has an opportunity to talk about his area of interest. In small groups those who share the same interest area can begin to delineate the facets they want to pursue. One group of eighty, refusing to delegate the job to a committee, held three "finding" meetings and came up with seven study groups on such a wide range of subjects as the Synoptic Gospels, the Creed, the sacraments, the doctrine of man, and Christian forgiveness. This group's identification with the results was demonstrated by its subsequent participation in the seven groups.

A planning or steering committee is another way in which groups can do a better job than an individual program chairman. The committee should, of course, be representative of the group for which the programs are being planned.

Members of the committee can interview a sampling of potential participants, in person preferably, but, if necessary, by telephone. It is usually helpful to type up a few "pump primers" as proposed topics to start their thinking. Be sure that the people interviewed are typical and representative of the whole group you hope to involve.

In parish groups it is possible to distribute mimeographed sheets at an early meeting with five or more topic choices to be rated in order of preference and with blank spaces for new suggestions.

At the first meeting in a series it is possible to take an interest census. Break the group into huddles of six. Ask each to appoint a leader, who will report back. They talk together for ten minutes and decide on one or two subjects of interest to them. The chairman then writes these on the blackboard.

One of the best ways to find interests is the use of PMR's (post meeting reaction sheets) or opinion blanks at the end of each meeting, at which time participants are asked to evaluate the meeting and make suggestions.

Suggestion boxes are widely and successfully used in industry. The use of such a box at the rear of the church could be surprisingly helpful, although at first people would have to be reminded and encouraged to use it.

Questionnaires can be used, but are not generally advised, in parish work. They are too impersonal, people don't like them, and the results are not sufficiently edifying or useful.

Avoid These Pitfalls

1. Letting one or two people do all the planning;
2. Paying too much attention to what people need and not enough to what interests them;
3. Failing to begin "where people are" (in terms of both knowledge and emotions);
4. Neglecting to do planning well in advance;
5. Sampling, interviewing, or calling on the old stand-bys all the time.

Step Two: Selecting the Topics

Selecting the topic is the process in which the planning committee discusses the general interest area that has been discovered in Step One and breaks it down into detailed topics. This is often mistaken to mean merely choosing a title for the meeting. It is somewhat like making a rough outline after the subject of a theme has been chosen. Only after these detailed topics have been found and grouped together, is the committee ready to phrase a suitable and appealing meeting *title.*

How to Select Topics

To break down the interest area into topics for one or more meetings is not difficult, but it does require patience and imagination on the part of the planning group or committee. Each one has to ask himself, "What aspects of this subject would I like to hear discussed?"

As each one states such a point, it is listed on the blackboard or on newsprint for all to see. Seeing these random items reminds him or others of additional points that need consideration. Such a committee meeting is not unlike the "brainstorming" sessions that are now so popular in industry. The idea is to get a lot of items down without pausing for a lengthy discussion of each one or of its relation to the others. When the group has exhausted its ideas, and only then, is it time to classify and arrange them and to fill in gaps.

An Example

A planning committee has found that there is interest in having a meeting on the general subject "Christian Family Discipline for Young Churchmen."

The following items were jotted down:

- The main causes of friction
- Good and bad methods of punishment
- The implications of the Christian doctrine of man
- The main needs for discipline:
  - Studies
  - Family chores
  - Spending money
- Self-discipline, and independence, how much?
- Parental authority, its origin and limits
- Church authority
  - The concept of freedom and authority in the Church
- Community and peer-group customs
  - Can we insist on behavior different from that of our social or community group?

How can we avoid arbitrary, erratic discipline?

- Our failings as parents. We are sinners too.
- Good and bad methods of punishment

Forgiveness and a new beginning

Choosing an Appealing Title

Once the general interest area and detailed topics have been found, it becomes necessary to find an appealing title for the meeting or series of meetings. Suppose, for instance, that the general topic is "The Use of the Prayer Book." A catchier and more appealing title is "The Prayer

Book Speaks in Our Uncertain Age." A comparative list of meeting titles follows. Note that those in the second listing have at least two merits over the "bad" ones, namely that they are more descriptive and more related to the "nowness" of the Christian's life.

Bad

Prayer Book History
Corporate Worship
Temptation, Sin and Suffering
Daily Prayer

Good

The Struggle for the Prayer Book
Power for Living from Worship
Our Difficulties as Christians
How to Say Your Prayers with the Prayer Book

Avoid These Pitfalls

1. Failing to set the ideas before the group. This job can be done on a blackboard or a large sheet of paper (attached to the wall with masking tape) and a crayon. This aids efficient and purposeful discussion and is essential in creative planning;

2. Confusing the exploration of suitable *topics* (parts of interest areas) with selecting *meeting titles*;

3. Wasting time in committee discussing the *answers* to problems when the main task is to *find* problems of interest and pose questions for the meeting;

4. Not giving enough time and effort to finding informative and appealing meeting titles;

5. Getting involved in a discussion of available resources of suitable group methods before Step Two and Step Three are adequately clarified.

Step Three: Defining Aims

Setting specific aims or purposes for a meeting is probably the most neglected phase of program planning. It is the key to successful planning. This is clear enough in everyday life: we choose tools after we know what kind of job we have to do; we select road maps and investigate the details of the route or alternate routes *after* we have decided where we want to go. In this case, as in program planning, not only is the final destination important, but so are our feelings and emotions. Do we want to go straight through at top speed, or do we want to take a pleasant vacation trip, enjoy the countryside and sights along the way and perhaps stop to visit friends or relatives? Shall we camp out or stay in motels? The trip is planned differently in each case.

In program planning, if we don't first set aims, we cannot choose the best resources for a given topic. Until we know what *resources* are available (Step 4), we cannot choose the most effective *group methods or procedures* (Step 5). Program planning has its own inherent logic.

Carefully discussing aims, before going on to the detailed planning of a meeting, focuses our attention on the real reason for holding the meeting in the first place. A rough idea of aim or purpose is always in the back of peoples' minds, and, usually, there it stays. Most groups are willing to settle for these vague hunches and object to spending time trying to make them clear, definite, and generally agreed upon. To them it seems like a waste of time.

Clarifying aims makes for more interesting meetings, meetings that achieve the purposes of the sponsoring organization, and it is also a necessary preliminary to *evaluation* of the meeting once it has occurred. Comparing what actually happened with what the committee hoped would happen—and finding reasons for the difference—is a key step toward *improving future programs.* For example, in the early days an automobile engine could be improved by mere tinkering. The great advances in recent years have come about by comparing performance with physical and chemical theory and then varying factors in order to approach theoretical maximum efficiency as closely as possible. Today, random tinkering by hunch, instead of engineering knowledge and evaluation, would get us nowhere. Evaluation is just as important in good program planning.

Some may ask, "If setting aims is so important and so primary, why is it not recommended as Step One?" The answer hinges upon theology and experience. The Church, knowing the faith and the deepest needs of men and women, could readily define aims and set up programs without consulting anyone. (In fact, many leaders do this.) But for maximum *effectiveness* in teaching adults, experience shows that it is essential to build programs around their areas of interest and with their participation. Once these areas have been found, worthwhile aims for specific meetings can be worked out that will satisfy both the individual participants and the long-term teaching strategy of the Church. Therefore Step One: *Finding Interests* and Step Two: *Selecting the Topics* must precede Step Three: *Defining Aims.*

When a committee is at work on Step Two, some ideas that actually belong in Step Three will probably be expressed and written on the blackboard. This is nothing to worry about; keep attention focused on the main task. Ideas cannot be forced out in logical sequence; they come out at random and later have to be classified and put in order.

How to Define Aims

The chairman should call on the planning or steering committee *to set down on the blackboard* a few ideas of what it hopes to accomplish in the program that is being planned. As the first casual ideas are discussed, it will be found that some may be combined and new ones will appear. Aims that are finally accepted by the group should be specific and attainable. Such long-range aims as "learning to become better Christians" are too general to give direction to a program. A record of the aims should be kept to aid in choosing resources (Step Four) and group processes (Step Five).

Here is an example of the aims for one of the sessions of a three-unit adult study course, "Creative Choices in Life."

Meeting title: *Finding and Using Your Talents*

1. To explore the factors people usually consider in choosing a career;
2. To realize the inadequacy of these standards;
3. To see the bearing of the Christian doctrine of judgment and the concept of Christian stewardship on the choice of a career and on the use of one's talents;

4. To begin to reexamine one's own life and career in the light of this teaching.

5. To get specific suggestions for helping to guide one's children;

6. To have the group participate actively in solving these problems instead of merely being "told the answers";

7. To raise some unresolved questions that will lead the group to read the short pamphlet provided.

Avoid These Pitfalls

1. Feeling that aims are obvious to everyone and not worth the effort of discussing and writing down;

2. Neglecting to have the participants review and accept the aims as their own before proceeding;

3. Doing a hasty, superficial job;

4. Setting aims that are too vague or too long-range to:
   (a) give direction to the planning, and
   (b) serve as a basis for evaluation of the meeting afterward.

Step Four: Uncovering Resources

Resources are the principal channel through which the group acquires new information. There are many kinds of resources: *people*—the clergy, speakers, or experts, persons in the group who have latent information which needs only to be brought into focus; *printed materials*—books, pamphlets, magazine articles, stories, newspaper clippings; *audio-visual materials*—movies (in whole or in part), video-taped presentations, film strips, slides, records, tape recordings, audio cassettes, informal dramatic skits. Printed materials, if brief, can be read to the group and well-chosen selections can be mimeographed easily. Remarkably thought-provoking material can be provided in this way. (Mimeographing or photocopying materials from books, pamphlets, or other sources may be an infringement of the copyright laws. Check with the publisher to secure permission before reproducing any material.) Church groups most frequently rely on resource *people*, avoiding printed or mimeographed material, and especially audio-visual material.

Any parish that is taking seriously its job of teaching the faith to adults should have an active parish library.

That is, it should have a well-rounded collection under the care of a volunteer librarian who not only knows where the books are but also is familiar with their contents. The parish library should have as complete an index as possible of pamphlets, films, film strips and recordings published in recent years by denominational headquarters, denominational and other religious presses, and by the National Council of the Churches of Christ. Such a library would be the number one source of printed material.

The public library can also be useful. A good librarian is usually full of suggestions and will have available indices such as the *Reader's Guide to Periodical Literature* and *Books in Print*. There are film catalogs and, frequently, lists of local experts and speakers. Today many public libraries have film departments, lending out 16 mm. documentary films, and most have record departments.

Start Well in Advance

It often seems that the easiest resource to use is a speaker. This is true only if he is merely invited to speak, without being briefed on the needs of your group and the goals of the meeting. This advance preparation takes time and effort. *In fact all good resources require time and effort to find and prepare them.* This is especially true of printed materials which need to be selected and mimeographed, and of audio-visual materials. One or more members of the steering committee can be delegated to do the exploration and then report to the committee with the resources they recommend.

Avoid These Pitfalls

1. Forgetting that resources are the principal channel through which the group acquires *new information* or tests decisions already made;

2. Keeping only topics in mind and forgetting aims while searching for resources;

3. Thinking of resources exclusively in terms of speakers or experts;

4. Not realizing that choice of resource can make or break a meeting;

5. Not being aware that *variety* of resources can add much to the interest and impact of a meeting or series of meetings.

Step Five: Choosing Effective Group Procedures

A group procedure is a way in which leaders or experts and participants can interact effectively in their examination of a problem of mutual interest. A group procedure is a way of using the resources found in Step Four.

There are many group procedures (methods and techniques) that have been found valuable. The small book *Adult Education Procedures: Manual for Group Discussion Participants* by Bergevin and Morris (see page 59) outlines very usable material. Some of the more widely used are the speech-forum, the symposium-forum, the panel-forum, the seminar, the small group discussion, the use of "discussion statements" prepared in advance, and the huddle (or buzz group). These ways of presenting information and having the participants react to it are very flexible and can be combined and modified to suit the needs of any particular meeting.

Group procedures can be learned from the printed page, but this is obviously not the best way. The best way is to have seen them in action and to have participated yourself. Actually, however, most readers will find on careful examination of *A Manual for Group Discussion Participants* (see p. 60) that they have experienced most of these procedures at one time or another, either in church groups or in various public meetings.

Program planners need especially to know the reasons for using one or another of the group procedures. Selecting the most effective group procedure for a given meeting affects adult learning more than any other single factor. A meeting on the same topic with the same resources can be a dismal failure with one group process and a resounding success with a more suitable process. All group procedures have this in common: they facilitate active participation by the group members in thinking about the subject, stating their own opinions, and asking questions. They thus contribute to solid rather than superficial learning. It is worth the expenditure of time and effort on the part of the planning committee to select the best one or the best combination.

Important factors to consider in choosing group procedures, apart from these already discussed in Steps One through Four, are the size of the group, the availability of discussion leaders for small groups, the amount of time available, whether the group needs much new information or needs principally to organize and think through what it already has. Physical factors are often crucial: the size of the room, its acoustics, the availability of other rooms in which small groups can meet temporarily, and whether or not the chairs are movable and can be rearranged readily.

How to Choose Group Procedures

First, the committee should list the resources and the group procedures that seem most likely for the program being planned. The task is to weave the best resources and group procedures into a logical sequence. To do this, block out the program in several ways, trying different combinations until one is found that utilizes most effectively the resources and best meets the goals. The following example [adapted from *Guide to Program Planning* by John McKinley and Robert M. Smith] shows how one planning committee blocked out a program and placed the parts in logical order.

Meeting Topic: *The Why's and How's of Family Worship*

Aims:

To explore the kinds of worship family members can share in the home;
To encourage family worship;
To get at some of the obstacles to family worship;
To to find out whether we need more programs on this topic, and, if so, what should be covered;
To get everyone to take an active part in the meeting.

Possible Resources:

1 film (20 min.), shows a family worshiping together in the home and celebrating such seasons as Advent and Epiphany;
4 panelists: a priest, a director of Christian education, a man who is an "old" churchman, a woman who is a recent convert;
1 pamphlet on devotional resources for family worship;
2 books: one on the meaning of prayer and one on

family worship services for use throughout the church year.

The experience of the audience.

Possible Group Procedures:

Speech-forum, *i.e.*, an address followed by a discussion;

Panel-forum, *i.e.*, experts discuss subject and group members address questions to them;

Symposium-forum, *i.e.*, experts each speak on one aspect of subject, followed by discussion;

Group discussion—sometimes a small discussion group meeting for only ten minutes is referred to as a huddle or buzz group.

The planners blocked out four program formats, finally deciding on Plan 3 for the reasons shown below.

Plan 1

Film

Panel (experts discuss film)

Forum (audience asks questions of the experts)

Plan 2

Film

Symposium (experts each speak on an aspect of the film)

Forum (audience asks questions of experts)

Plan 3

Film

Small group discussions (groups of 10-15 persons for 30 minutes discuss film and form questions for experts)

Forum (experts answer questions from groups and invite open discussion)

Plan 4

Film

Panel (discusses film briefly)

Huddles (10 minute group discussion to identify questions only)

Forum (questions answered by experts)

Pamphlets can be given out at any of the programs.

Some Reasons for Choosing Plan 3

Thirty-minute group discussions (rather than ten-minute huddle sessions) were preferred because group members had much to share and compare. The experience of parents was considered a valuable resource. The experts in Plan 3 were used to clarify phases of the subject based on their unique experience.

Group discussion (rather than huddles) would set the stage for a freer discussion in forum.

Plan 4 puts off parents' problems for most of the program. The discussion of the film by experts may hamper the free participation of the parents.

Plans 1 and 2 do not provide for enough parent participation on a topic of great interest to them.

Avoid These Pitfalls

1. Sticking to one or two favorite or familiar group procedures instead of learning them all and selecting the most appropriate ones;
2. Overlooking the specified goals when choosing group procedures;
3. Forgetting that the main purpose of any group procedure is to get active participation and interaction by the group members;
4. Ignoring the physical arrangements of the meeting place;
5. Failing to take the participant's knowledge, limitations, background, *etc.*, into consideration.

Step Six: Outlining the Program in Detail

After the basic parts of the program have been determined, the program should be laid out in detail and the various responsibilities assigned.

The various parts of the program should be put into a time schedule that makes room for the basic resources and methods as well as for the information and directions which the participants will need to know. Therefore, several decisions have to be made before the program is complete: (1) What information should be supplied to the participants prior to and at different times during the meeting by the chairman? (2) Who will do the necessary jobs, such as arranging the room setup, serving as chairman, leader, and recorder? (3) Should the participants evaluate all or part of the program, and, if so, how?

In the course of any program the participants should be told:

The purpose of the program
- What is the topic?
- Why does the planning group consider it worthwhile?
- How does it relate to previous or subsequent programs?

How the program will unfold
- What basic parts will there be?
- Will there be an intermission or break?
- At what time will the session end and will refreshments be served?

What is expected of them
- What can they hope to gain?
- How and when are they expected to participate?

The purpose of each resource used

The names and qualifications of the resource persons and materials

The Timetable

Each element in the program should be scheduled to begin and end at a specific time. The persons staging the program should adhere to the timetable insofar as this is practical. Of course, the chairman should use common sense. Participant reaction and the general "feel" of the meeting may cause him to make adjustments. Though the timetable may not be followed strictly, it is almost always best to end the program at the agreed time.

A Sample Timetable

8:00 Chairman introduces the program topic and why important,
Procedure to be followed,
What is expected of audience.

8:05 Chairman (or a second person) introduces the film:
Title and length,
Why being used,
What to look for.

8:10 *Film* is presented.

8:30 Chairman sets up discussion groups and gives them their instructions.

8:35 *Discussion groups* meet. (Pencils and paper are available; discussion leaders have previewed film and prepared questions for discussion.)

9:00 *Forum.* Discussion leaders (or recorders) present summaries and submit questions to panel for comments and answers. Participants join in after a time with questions and comments.

9:25 Chairman summarizes the program.

9:30 Chairman ends the session.

Jobs to be Filled

The committee will need to line up persons for the specific duties that concern the program. Spreading out responsibility will make for interest on the part of many and will guard against overworking one or two persons. Specific duties in the following areas should be agreed on:

1. Jobs: discussion leaders, recorders, moderators (Review duties and a check list in a book like *A Manual for Group Discussion Participants.* See p. 60.)

2. Physical setup: tables, chairs, ash trays, name cards, pencils, notepaper, blackboard, chalk, screen and audio-visual equipment.

3. Publicity: printed or mimeographed, newspapers, announcement by clergy, telephone.

4. Advising resource persons of specific needs the program is attempting to meet.

Evaluation

It is important to evaluate any program, as discussed previously under *Aims* (Step Three). It is not always necessary to involve the participants directly in the evaluation. Some ways of getting audience reaction are:

Observation by the planning committee or by assigned observers,

Selected interviews,

Use of opinion blanks,

Discussion groups—instructed to come up with criticism and recommendations.

The important thing to decide on is the *degree to which the aims were met.*

Avoid These Pitfalls

1. Failing to tell moderators and speakers, panel members, *etc.* what they are to do and how much time they have to do it in.

2. Failing to tell moderators and speakers how their presentation relates to the program as a whole;

3. Sticking unnecessarily close, or not close enough, to the timetable;

4. Not letting participants know what is expected of them.

Note: Some of the material in this chapter appeared in a booklet of the same title written by the author and Dr. Theodore M. Switz. Although skeletal, it represents, in a revised form, the commonly recognized elements in program planning. A more detailed coverage has been done by Bergevin, Morris, and Smith, *Adult Education Procedures.* For reference to this book, see page 59.

9. A METHOD OF SMALL GROUP BIBLE STUDY

The Approach to Bible Study

THERE ARE many approaches to Bible study. The Bible can be read as literature. It can be studied as a historical document. It can be investigated to determine the basis of the Church's teachings. The method we use depends upon the objective we wish to reach. The objective of group Bible study is to gain insight into the relevance of God's mighty acts, as revealed through Holy Scripture, in our lives, the life of the Church, or in relation to a particular task which we are undertaking in the name of the Church. As we rely upon corporate worship and the sacramental life to guide us, so we rely upon the Bible.

Persons gathered together in a community—the group—are confronted by God's revelation of himself as that revelation is communicated through the Bible in the interrelation among members of the group. The Bible, like the Church, is more than a record of God's revelation in the past. It, like the Church, is also a means whereby we become aware of him in terms of the here and now of our lives. It is this element of the here and now, in which the *relevance* of God's acts to our own lives is seen, that particularly commends to the Church an approach such as this.

When we approach the Bible, we ought to keep in mind the following facts:

First, THE BIBLE IS AT THE SAME TIME WORD OF GOD AND HUMAN WORD. The Bible is not simply "Word of God." It is not a collection of inspired texts which we may use and apply to ourselves irrespective of their context and historical background.

The Bible is not simply "Word of man." It is not a book among other books, giving an account of events, the meaning of which we understand from studying the historical circumstances.

The whole Bible, Old and New Testaments and the Apocrypha, is a unity, bears witness to God's revelation of himself in Jesus Christ, and cannot be understood apart from him.

Second, IN THE BIBLE, HISTORY IS SEEN IN THE PERSPECTIVE OF ETERNITY, WHICH ALONE GIVES MEANING TO TEMPORAL EVENTS. The Bible can best be described as a drama happening in history, with a prologue (Creation and Paradise) and an epilogue (Vision of the Kingdom to Come) beyond history. We must keep in mind this constant tension between things temporal and things eternal.

Third, THE BIBLE IS A TESTIMONY OF A COMMUNITY TO A COMMUNITY. The Spirit of Truth is promised, not to each individual going his own way, but to the community of believers. Whenever we approach the Bible it is as members of a community, the Church, by which community the New Testament was produced and the Old Testament used and preserved as part of our heritage. So it is in our personal, devotional reading of the Bible.

Certain things are given us as a group which we would probably never have discovered alone. A special promise and blessing of Christ rests on those who gather in his name, "for where two or three are gathered in my name, there am I in the midst of them." New insights and new understandings come to those who gather in his name for the purpose of studying the Bible.

Fourth, BIBLE STUDY AND PRAYER ARE INSEPARABLE. Jesus Christ alone can open our minds to hear his Word and to accept it in faith and obedience. We must leave behind preconceived ideas and approach the Bible ready to listen, in an expectant attitude. Where God speaks, something happens. "For the word of God is living and active, sharper than any two-edged sword . . . discerning the thoughts and intentions of the heart." When we allow ourselves to be searched and questioned, only then does the Bible unfold its mystery. We come with our anxious questions, God's word reaches us, and then, as we are quiet and listen, God asks us the real questions. Adam in the garden had to have ears to hear God's question, "Where are you?" In prayerful listening to God's word we discover our real needs. Bible study offers one of the ways in which we can be led to a personal encounter with Jesus Christ himself.

Conduct of the Meetings

First, gather together a small group of "interested seekers." All people are not interested in studying the Bible; start with those who are. The group should not be larger than twelve or fourteen, nor is it advisable to start with less than three or four. This is a fruitful experience for husbands and wives to share with other married couples.

Second, meet regularly, at a particular place, for an agreed-upon length of time. It has been found that groups that meet regularly stay together. It is best to meet not less than once every two weeks and not more than once a week. Some groups find it best to move from home to home, whereas others prefer to meet outside the home. Start your group study promptly at the agreed-upon hour and close your meeting at an early hour. Most groups have found from eight to ten o'clock in the evening the most convenient time, with an hour and a half devoted to Bible study and a half hour for fellowship before breaking up.

Third, open the Bible study session by devoting ten

to twelve minutes to silent reading and rereading of the Bible passage. (The Bible passage should be selected at least one meeting in advance of its study so that each person can prepare at home for the group study.)

The host or chairman for the meeting should call the group to order, announce clearly the passage to be studied (seeing that each person finds the passage), indicate when it is time to start the silent reading period, and close the silent reading period by opening the discussion. It is recommended that the chairman present a brief introduction to the passage, giving its context in Scripture and indicating the main theme of the passage.

Fourth, allow for free discussion of the passage by the whole group without permitting the study to disintegrate. Don't be alarmed when the discussion proves difficult. There may be cold silences and periods of heated debate when free, open discussion is allowed, but it is through this very expression of freedom that God speaks to us. The chairman should keep the group digging at the meaning of the passage without driving the group and without allowing the discussion to dissipate itself. Two questions have been found helpful in leading open discussions:

What is the passage saying?

What is the passage saying to you or to us?

The chairman can use these two questions to stimulate discussion and at the same time give it direction. After an hour, or an hour and a quarter, it has been found helpful for the chairman to ask a member of the group to sum up the discussion. The chairman then assigns the passage for study at the next meeting before closing the period with prayers.

Fifth, the prayer period which concludes the session should be undertaken in the same spirit as the Bible study, allowing members of the group to participate in the prayers. Group prayer is difficult. Many groups have found that it helps if the chairman opens the prayer period by reading a prayer or collect which the whole group can join in saying. Each prayer period should allow for silent corporate prayer and a period during which any member of the group can offer his own prayer or ask the prayers of the group for anyone or for himself.

The chairman ends the prayer period with a prayer or two and a grace. Occasionally, it is good to allow time from the Bible study to discuss the meaning of the prayer period. Prayers should not be allowed to become automatic and mechanical.

It is good to have a cup of coffee or other refreshments, but keep refreshments simple. Break up the session early.

Preparation for Group Study of the Bible

Each member of a Bible study group should prepare at home for the meeting of the group. The need for preparation will increase as the group matures. This home study should begin with a careful reading of the Bible passage assigned to make quite sure of its meaning. Parallels should be looked up and, if possible, compared with different translations. Then the following questions should be asked:

1. What is the relation of this passage to its content and setting? Who is speaking, who is addressed, and what are the circumstances?
2. What does it say about God: His attitude toward the people at that time, his attitude toward man *now*?
3. What are the difficult words—difficult because they are not understood, or because they have been heard so often that they have lost their meaning for men today? (The reader should try to find the main passages which throw light on the meaning of these words, and try to translate them into everyday language.)
4. Can this truth be illustrated from the contemporary situation in the world and from the life of the Church today?

Where to Begin

The Bible is a difficult book to begin to study. Group study is the method which is close to the manner in which Christians originally received the word of God and have mantained their encounter with God's word through the centuries. Here we are concerned with where in the Bible to begin.

The experience of several parishes that have begun group study of the Bible has demonstrated that the first chapter of Genesis is not the place to begin. We should begin where we are. Because we are New Testament people, we should begin with the New Testament. We read the whole Bible, Old and New Testaments, as Christians, and it is important for us to commence with a study of our New Testament beginnings. Before too long a Bible study group will be forced to take up a serious study of the Old Testament. In the meantime, where to begin in the New Testament?

The exact chapter and verse to open a group study of the Bible should be determined largely by the nature of the group itself. The group should be consulted and should make its own decisions as to where to begin. The following considerations may help.

Although some will want to begin with one of the Gospels because of their conspicuous importance, experience has shown that the Gospels are a difficult place to start group study. The Gospels were not the first books of the New Testament to be written for the reason that the message of the Gospel was carried by the personal witness of the Apostolic Church through an oral tradition. The Gospels were written later to preserve their message in its Apostolic form. Because the first experience of Christians is that of coming into the Christian community, it may be better to begin group Bible study with one of the Epistles. The form and message of the letters are oriented to the struggle of the people to be the Church. Therefore, they are closer to our mood and mind when we are in the beginning steps of becoming a fellowship (or group).

If, however, the group decides to begin with one of the Gospels, it would be well to start with Matthew, Mark, or Luke rather than with John. Perhaps the Gospel of Mark might offer the best opportunity for getting into the Bible, as it is in some ways the simplest and most direct. If the group decision is to begin with the Epistles, one of the shorter and less complicated letters of Paul—Galatians or Philippians—would be a wise choice.

Use of Outlines

After having completed eight to twelve sessions, the group should be capable of directing its course through the Bible with the help of such commentaries and outlines as Suzanne de Dietrich's *The Witnessing Community* (Westminster), or Bernhard W. Anderson's *The Unfolding Drama of the Bible* (Association Press).

One of the important factors in initiating group Bible study is that the group become a concerned fellowship in which each member is given opportunity to participate. This is difficult and will depend largely upon the growth of interpersonal freedom within the group. The Bible becomes the living Word of God when human beings submit themselves to its authority in their lives through the meetings and partings of the members of the group.

Bibliography for Group Bible Study

Bible Translations:

It is best, in group Bible study, to use one translation in the group, but it is a real help to use two or more translations in home preparation.

The Holy Bible, Revised Standard Version (New York: Thomas Nelson and Sons, 1952).

The Holy Bible, King James Version, 1611. Various publishers.

The Holy Bible, American Standard Version (Various publishers, 1901).

Phillips, J. B., *Letters to Young Churches* (New York: The Macmillan Company, 1969 paper).

Phillips, J. B., *The Gospels* (New York: The Macmillan Company, 1961 paper).

The Common Bible, Revised Standard Version (New York: Collins, 1973).

Good News for Modern Man (American Bible Society, New York: 1966).

The Jerusalem Bible (Doubleday & Co., New York: 1967).

The New English Bible (Oxford University Press: 1970).

The New American Bible (Various publishers, 1970).

Commentaries:

Do not use commentaries in the meeting of the group for Bible study. Their use should be restricted to home preparation.

Interpreter's Bible, Ed. George A. Buttrick (Nashville: Abingdon Press).

Abingdon Bible Commentary, David Downey et al. (Nashville: Abingdon Press).

The Daily Bible Study Series, Commentaries on New Testament Books, William Barclay (Philadelphia: Westminster Press).
Tyndale New Testament Commentaries. (Grand Rapids: Wm. B. Eerdmans Publishing Co.)
Young's Analytical Concordance to the Bible. (Grand Rapids: Wm. B. Eerdmans Publishing Co.)

Books on the Bible:

Reading books on the Bible is in no way a substitute for reading the Bible itself. Use the following suggested books for help in getting into the Bible itself.

Anderson, Bernhard W., *The Unfolding Drama of the Bible.* New York: Association Press, 1957 rev. ed.
Dentan, Robert C., *The Apocrypha: Bridge of the Testaments.* New York: The Seabury Press, 1954.
Dentan, Robert C., *The Holy Scriptures: A Survey.* New York: The Seabury Press, 1952.

THE DIVINE DRAMA OF HUMAN REDEMPTION

The story of what God has done and what he is waiting to do to help us is called in theology *The Drama of Redemption* and is set forth in the Bible. It can be simply understood as a series of five great acts which God has done for us. Usually, we think that the Bible is relating something that happened a long time ago. Actually, it is the eternal story of God and every human life. It is the drama of God and us. It deals with our personal life at this very moment. What God has done to help us can be ours right *now.*

In Act One—God Created Us—Sin Separated Us.

Act I of the drama tells how God created us in his image to live in fellowship with him and with other people. It tells how he gave us the gift of life and how we became living persons. We are creatures made by him. But we are different from all other things God made in that we have freedom to make choices. Every person has the freedom to rebel against God. When we rebel we create a state of separation from him. This separation causes inner turmoil, anxiety, loneliness, frustration, and insecurity.

In Act Two—God Taught Us The Law.

Act II of the drama tells what God has done to teach us how to live with him and with other men. It is the story of all those things, related in the Old Testament, that God has done to teach us the Laws of the Good Life. It is conveniently summarized in the *Ten Commandments,* but in many different ways "the Law" is taught in much of the Old Testament. The great Hebrew prophets such as Amos and Isaiah clarified the spiritual meaning of the Hebrew Law. It is in their teaching that we find it in its highest form, until we come to the *Sermon on the Mount* in the New Testament.

However, there is a vast difference between *knowing* what is right and being able to *do* what is right. Mere knowledge of God's law can't help us. Our separation from God prevents us from doing right. Our sin is our basic problem, not our ignorance of what we ought to do. The Law serves to increase our knowledge of our own sinfulness. After we have known all that there is to know about right and wrong we still need a Savior to redeem us from our state of separation.

In Act Three—God Became a Man and Died for Us.

Act III is that part of the great drama of God's mighty acts in which he became a man like us. In theology, this act is called the *Incarnation.* Here God is not merely telling us how to live. He lived our life within the same physical and mental limitations in which we live it. He met our temptations and overcame them. He lived through all our human problems and clarified them. He suffered rejection, loneliness, misunderstanding, physical pain, and finally death itself. He demonstrated his tremendous love for us. He showed what could be made out of life lived completely in accordance with his will. By his *Resurrection,* he showed conclusively that death is not the end of everything. This made possible a new kind of relationship with God, which no academic teaching about "how to live" could ever produce. As a result, when anyone recognizes God in the life of Jesus Christ and is moved by gratitude and trust to have faith in him, he enters into this new and wonderful relationship. It brings with it strength to face life's burdens and power to live properly with others. It heals our separation from God and from other people. We are reconciled; the process of salvation has begun.

In Act Four—God Sent Us The Church.

Act IV is the mighty act by which God created the Church. What God did two thousand years ago in the lives of the twelve Apostles needed a means by which it could be made available to other men then and now. You and I can only know what can be done to change our lives by being made a part of a group in which his new life is understood and made tangible. This group is the Church. We enter it by Baptism when the Church intends that we be incorporated into a structure of relationships that include a truly Christian family and a truly Christian parish. Through these new relationships we come to know Jesus as our Lord and Savior, and we come to share in his Holy Spirit, who gives us a strength that is not our own. As we receive the Spirit we acquire the power to become new creatures and live a new kind of life.

In Act Five—God Will Come To Judge Us.

Act V of the drama tells us what the ultimate purpose of this life is. We learn that there is a life beyond death. We learn that a time will come when each one of us will be judged by Jesus Christ. We learn that the major question involved in our judgment will be, *Are you able to live in loving relationship with God and others eternally?*

If we are the kind of persons who are able truly to be with God eternally we shall enter *Heaven.* If we still have no desire or capacity for relationship with God and with others, he will allow us to be separated eternally from him. Hell is eternal separation and loneliness of our own choosing.

By these five Acts—*Creation, Lawgiving, Incarnation, Sending the Holy Spirit,* and the *Judgment,* God has entered our lives to save us from sin and separation, from loneliness and frustration. This is the Good News of the Gospel.

The Mighty Acts of God in

THE DIVINE DRAMA OF HUMAN REDEMPTION

As set forth in the Bible

ACT I	ACT II	ACT III	ACT IV	ACT V
God presented in the role of	God presented in the role of	God presented in the role of	God presented in the role of	God presented in the role of
CREATOR →	**GOVERNOR** →	**REDEEMER** →	**SANCTIFIER** →	**JUDGE**
↓	↓	↓	↓	↓
Symbolized in the action of	Symbolized in the action of	Symbolized in the action of	Symbolized in the action of	Symbolized in the action of
INBREATHING →	**INSPIRATION** →	**INCARNATION** →	**INDWELLING** →	**COMING AGAIN**
Adam	Law Givers and Prophets	Jesus, the Cross, Resurrection, and Ascension	The Holy Spirit in the Church, a colony of Heaven	The General Resurrection and Last Judgment
↓ ↓ ↓	↓	↓	↓	↓
Man a **CREATURE** → With power of choice and rebellion	Man a **SINNER** → Who cannot save himself	Man a **REDEEMED SINNER** → to live in Relationship	Man, a new **CREATURE IN CHRIST,** → living under Judgment	Man enters finally into the **HEAVENLY CITIZENSHIP**
		OR		**OR**
		a persistent Rebel →	→	God permits man to go to his own place: HELL

This drama differs from a stage show in that:

— It really happened and is always happening.
— Every man is a participant whether he wills so or not.
— All the acts are being presented at the same time.
— Part of this drama is "in time" — part "above time."
— The Prayer Book and the Creeds epitomize this drama for us.